Internationalizing
THE COMMUNITY COLLEGE

EDITED BY
RICHARD M. ROMANO

Community College Press®
a division of the American Association of Community Colleges
Washington, D.C.

Internationalizing
THE COMMUNITY COLLEGE

NORTHWEST VISTA COLLEGE

The American Association of Community Colleges (AACC) is the primary advocacy organization for the nation's community colleges. The association represents 1,100 two-year, associate degree-granting institutions and more than 10 million students. AACC promotes community colleges through six strategic action areas: national and international recognition and advocacy for community colleges, learning and accountability, leadership development, economic and workforce development, connectedness across AACC membership, and international and intercultural education. Information about AACC and community colleges may be found at www.aacc.nche.edu.

© 2002 American Association of Community Colleges

Community College Press
American Association of Community Colleges
One Dupont Circle, NW
Suite 410
Washington, DC 20036

Printed in the United States of America.

ISBN 0-87117-349-2

Contents

FOREWORD

Kent A. Farnsworth
Crowder College, Missouri

A friend who grew up in a small town in the White Mountains of southern Arizona once told me a story about his father that has helped me place the September 11, 2001, terrorist attack against the United States in a personal context. As a boy, my friend's father lived in a small cabin near the town's lumber mill. Earlier in his life, while his father was attending dental school in Chicago, the boy had wandered off and become lost in the city. His mother was so traumatized by the event that when the family moved to this cabin, with the forest stretching off in the distance as far as she could see, she insisted that a tall board fence be built around the backyard, where she placed the boy and told him to stay put. He turned out to be an ingenious little fellow, and it took him only a few days to scale the fence and head off into the forest—where again, he became lost.

The search for the boy went on throughout the day and eventually involved the entire town, but no one was able to find him. Finally, they enlisted the help of an old Mexican trapper who went off into the woods and within a few hours found the frightened and disoriented child and brought him back to his mother. In her joy and frustration, she assured the old man that her son would never get outside the fence again, to which the trapper replied, "As long as the boy is living inside the fence, he will never be safe. If you had spent the time it took to build the fence teaching the boy to live with the forest, how to cope with its dangers and problems, he wouldn't have become lost. If you want him to be able to survive in the world, he needs to learn how to live outside the fence."

Much to the mother's credit, she let the old trapper teach the boy how to find his way about in the woods. He showed him how to use the streams to find the river that flowed down to the lumber mill, and how to use a steam whistle that sounded regularly at the mill to orient himself, then track a straight line through the woods. After a final "test," the old man returned the boy to his mother, and, again to her credit, she had the board fence taken down and let the boy run. He was never lost again.

I have often used that story to point out how much we as Americans have grown up inside the fence. We know very little about the world beyond, and in most cases have done little to learn of the wonderful opportunities, much less how to cope with the dangers and problems, that exist there. But on September 11, the entire significance of the story changed for me. The fence was broken down, not by friends who wanted to enlarge my experience and extend my freedom, but by an enemy who wished to show that I was no longer completely safe, even inside the fence.

We have, it seems, two choices as to how we respond to this breach in our fence. We can build a stronger and taller fence, attempting to isolate ourselves more completely from the forest, its dangers and potentials, or we can determine that we will do what is necessary to understand the dangers, problems, and opportunities that life beyond the fence presents. In the long term, if we are to create a secure and peaceful world, our only choice is to learn to live beyond what are now self-imposed boundaries. But to do so will require effort in at least three directions on our part. We must become better informed as a nation, we must gain greater experience with and appreciation for those who live beyond the fence, and we must find ways for them to better understand and appreciate what we value and hope for in life.

Despite being the most information-rich society in the world, we are poorly informed, particularly when it comes to other peoples, cultures, and histories. I recently saw a list of questions that American tourists had purportedly asked park rangers at Colorado's Mesa Verde National Park, the site of ancient Anasazi cliff dwellings. The questions included, "Did people build these ruins, or did Indians?" "Why did they build their houses so close to the road?" "What did they worship in these kivas—their own made-up religion?" "Do you know about any undiscovered ruins?" "Why do you think the Indians decided to live in Colorado?"

Although these examples were selected because of their absurdity, they are symptomatic of both our cultural insensitivity and our lack of understanding of how other cultures fit into any kind of social and historical context. As a student of the Middle East and of the world's religions, I have been invited, since the events of September 11, to talk to groups about Islam, attitudes in the Near East, and the historical development of Afghanistan. I find that, despite the crying need for a new literacy in this country—a literacy based upon knowing about and understanding other cultures—we are a nation of cultural illiterates. Such realizations should send a clear message to the American educational community. Just as it has been our responsibility to provide the literacy of the three Rs and the literacy required by the age of computer technology, it now becomes our responsibility to help those with whom we work to develop a new international and multicultural literacy. To fail to do so leaves us wandering listlessly about, both within the fence and without, with no sense of what is happening to us and no informed way to respond.

Yet "information about" does not necessarily lead to understanding and appreciation. A number of years ago, in an effort to assess the effects on student attitudes of a World Religions course I teach, I developed a brief pre- and postassessment of multicultural appreciation and religious tolerance. To my amazement, while some in the class showed significant increases on the appreciation scale by the end of the course, an almost equal number showed equally significant decreases. I have repeated the survey over the course of several years with similar results. The only conclusion I can reach from the data is that students enter the class with predispositions about other peoples, religions, and cultures, and find what information they need in the course to reinforce their positive or negative attitudes. If that is indeed the case, changing multicultural attitudes in a positive way requires not just "information about," but some kind of personal "experience with," the new culture that exposes people to it on an emotional, rather than just an intellectual, level. We must as educators get our students out into the world and involved with other cultures at the "heart" level.

When my youngest sons reached an age of sufficient appreciation, I began to take one or both of them to another country each summer to spend a few weeks immersed in a new culture. In March 1999 my youngest son, Paul, then 15, accompanied a friend and me to Thailand, where the friend was interested in finding sources of gems coming into Thailand from neighboring Myanmar. Before going up into the villages along the Burmese border, we spent a few days in Bangkok and Chiang Mai, visiting floating markets, rafting down a river, and riding elephants through the jungle. For Paul, Thailand was a giant Epcot Center, with one exciting exotic adventure after another.

The last part of our journey took us to Mai Sot, a rural village separated from Myanmar only by a shallow, muddy river. Because of the political turmoil in Myanmar, thousands of Burmese refugees were crowded along the Thai side of the river in makeshift camps, and we found ourselves wandering among the lean-tos and the crude tents, looking at the crafts the refugees were making in an effort to support themselves. As we neared one small covered market, a small group of lepers approached, led by a woman in an advanced stage of the illness. Most of her fingers were gone, and her lips, nose, and ears had largely been eaten away. In one crippled arm she clutched a naked baby girl, bloated by starvation. The other stump of a hand she held out for alms. We gave her what loose money we had in our pockets and moved on through the market, but I noticed that Paul, who was usually a bundle of energy, had become quiet and subdued. "I had no idea people had to live like this," he said. "We really are lucky people, aren't we?"

This brief encounter on the Thai border changed him. He is a more thoughtful person and is aware of those about him who have less. Educators need to find ways to give every student that "experience with" so that when disasters like September 11 occur, we can shape our personal and national response using more than "information about," and can include the human element that comes only through direct experience with other peoples and their lives.

It seems equally important to me that we refuse to let the attack of September 11 cause us to seal ourselves in and close our doors to the rest of the world. Here we are, supposedly the best-informed society on the globe, but with little understanding of our global neighbors. Imagine how much less those who live in places where information is restricted by policy or poverty know about us! Our responsibility as educators is to bring the world to our students in whatever safe and manageable ways we can.

Shortly after relations were reestablished between the United States and Russia, our college hosted 10 Russian academics and business leaders for a week of immersion in American life, housing them with host families in the community. One morning was spent touring the local La-Z-Boy plant, where workers making the recliner chairs are paid based upon their productivity, with deductions for products that have to be reworked. It is one of the company's most productive plants. As we left the plant, one of the Russian businessmen said, "I have never seen people work so hard and so well. At last I understand why America has been so successful." No course in economics could have presented the lesson as effectively.

Even more significant was the scene at the host family's residence the following Saturday when I stopped to pick up the same businessman to take him to the airport. He left the family with hugs, a few tears, and assurances that he would keep in touch. I know from my association with the family that he has. They talk to each other by e-mail and occasional phone calls, sharing thoughts about what is happening in the world, not as Russians and Americans, but as two concerned families who want the best for themselves and for each other.

If little else positive comes from the horrible events of September 11, I believe the tragedy has at least convinced us as a nation that there are serious challenges facing us that we cannot resolve by ourselves. If we are ever to have peace in the world, it will not depend solely on finding and eliminating sources of terrorism, but on identifying and eliminating the root causes of the deep-seated differences that cause people to act so violently and irrationally. As American educators, perhaps we cannot do much to directly change the world of those who would count us as their enemies, but we can do a great deal to change our own. That is what this book is all about. All that remains now is for us to do it.

PREFACE

Richard M. Romano

"Toto, I have a feeling we're not in Kansas anymore."
—Dorothy in The Wizard of Oz

Each year the American Association of Community Colleges (AACC) devotes a special issue of the *Community College Journal* to international education. These issues are full of examples of how community colleges are expanding their involvement in global education. A recent one contains an essay by Kent A. Farnsworth that recalls his own transformation in thinking when, at the age of 14, he and his family moved to Iran for two years. Just as Dorothy realized when the cyclone hurled her into the world of Oz, Farnsworth discovered that he was no longer living in the isolated world he once knew. In relating this expanded view of the world to the community college, Farnsworth says:

> *From a purely economic [employment] standpoint, graduates who leave our institutions without multicultural experience will be severely handicapped. . . . But the greater value, in my view, comes from what developing a global perspective does to what and who we are as individuals . . . part of the learning process—of becoming an "educated" person—must now involve opening the lives and minds of students to the wonders of the new Oz. (Farnsworth 2001, 10–11)*

Whether it is students' minds they seek to open, or their job skills they propose to develop, U.S. institutions of higher education do not seem to be doing a very good job of producing graduates with global competency. A recent study by the American Council on Education documents the relatively low level of such competency among undergraduates from both two- and four-year colleges and states that "with few notable exceptions, efforts to internationalize have to date been more symbolic than real" (2000, 5).

The study highlights the "growing demand . . . for workers with international expertise" (both language and cross-cultural skills) (ACE, 3). This is contrasted with the "relatively few undergraduates [who] gain international or intercultural competence in college" (ACE, 1). As evidence of the deficiencies in this area, the study documents the decline in foreign language enrollments over the past 40 years from 16 percent of total enrollments in the 1960s to 8 percent from the mid-1970s to the present. It also documents the fact that only 3 percent of U.S. undergraduates study abroad, far short of the 10 percent goal set by President Clinton for the year 2000. Progress on internationalizing the curriculum is harder to document, but the study finds that in 1989, 70 percent of four-year college graduates, but only 21 percent of associate degree graduates, had at least one nonlanguage course with an international focus.

Looking at the report for some bright spots in the community college, we can say that study-abroad enrollments are up; the number of international students enrolling at community colleges is increasing at a faster rate than the national average; the number of two-year colleges that require languages for graduation increased from 18 percent in 1987 to 23 percent in 1995; and 10 percent of two-year colleges have grants or contracts focusing on international activities (ACE, 5–14).

Even with these promising trends, it is clear that far too little is being done to bring an international perspective to the community college, and that those who refuse to recognize their role in educating students so that they can live and work in the global village are preparing them for second-class citizenship. When pressed, most community colleges would no doubt agree with the rhetoric of international education, but too few back it up with the actions necessary to turn their "local colleges" into "global community colleges." The purpose of this book is to assist in that effort.

Focus of This Book

Few would deny that the forces of global change have had an impact on even the smallest of communities in the United States. The changing student demographics, the impact of information technologies, the impact of the media, and the training requirements of a more internationally competitive labor force have thrust some degree of globalization upon all of our colleges. These forces of change are skillfully described in a recent book by John Levin, *Globalizing the Community College* (2001). Levin examines the way in which the local orientation of the community college is penetrated by a global ideology that changes the college organizationally. Unlike Levin's book, this collection of essays does not adopt an overarching analytical theme. Rather, this book's primary objective is to serve as a practical guide for community colleges who wish to internationalize their campuses. It documents the growing involvement of selected community colleges in international education and invites others to participate in the process.

Efforts to internationalize the community college might involve the following elements: a curricular commitment to internationalism, faculty development, the development of study-abroad programs, the recruiting of international students to the campus, and extracurricular programs of an international/intercultural nature for both on- and off-campus groups. To assist them in the process of internationalizing, community colleges usually belong to one or more of the following national organizations: the American Council on International Intercultural Education (ACIIE); NAFSA:Association of International Educators; the College Consortium for International Studies (CCIS); and the Community Colleges for International Development (CCID). Several authors for this book were drawn from the leaders of these organizations.

A second objective of the book is to introduce colleges to ways in which they might use federal grants to finance some of these initiatives. One of the strategies for successful grant writing is to talk to those who have experience in this process. For that reason, four of the 13 chapters discuss grant-funded activities and were written by the people who developed and worked with the grant projects they are discussing. Again, the focus here is on activities that can be replicated, although not in exact detail, on other campuses. The last chapter deals directly with where the money can be found. If this book stimulates more interest in applying for international grants, it will have performed an important function.

Organization of Chapters

The chapters in this book cover all of the elements identified above as important to bringing an international perspective to the community college. Since most students will be exposed to international/intercultural issues through the curriculum, two of the chapters deal directly with curriculum development. Both are reports on how different federal grants have been used to bring a greater international perspective into the classroom. That is not to say that outside money is necessary for such a task. Clearly, most faculty modify their courses without any outside funding. Curriculum development is part of our job, and this is how it should be. Nevertheless, as the authors of this book can testify, outside funding helps push things along and brings an air of legitimacy to an effort that is not always fully recognized.

Besides curriculum development, the other major emphasis in the book is on the development of partnerships abroad. Three of the chapters are devoted to this area. Other chapters focus on study abroad, on international student recruitment, and on the development of English as a second language (ESL) and other programs for those students. None of these elements are mutually exclusive. For instance, partners abroad are used in study abroad and student exchange programs, for faculty and curriculum development, and for recruiting students. The mixture of these elements is evident from the titles of the chapters themselves.

In chapter 1, Donald A. Dellow gives a president's perspective on why community colleges should be involved in international education. He also shows how global competency can be achieved to a greater or lesser degree and suggests ways in which a community college can assist students in developing the highest degree of competency. His essay is a pep talk for internationalizing the campus and provides a rationale for the chapters that follow. Dellow argues that the effort pays dividends in terms of developing a more competent work-force; enriching the personal lives of students, faculty, and others in the community; and enhancing the revenue stream for the college.

In chapter 2, Robert Frost talks about recruiting international students. While little actual research has been done on the "art" of recruiting these students, insights and experiences are shared widely through conference forums and training workshops. Frost is a frequent presenter at these workshops, and his hands-on chapter summarizes many of the best practices he has encountered. In chapter 3, Scott Branks del Llano and Jeana Remington, from the Dallas Community College system, write about ESL and student services for international students. This is a necessary follow-up chapter to the one on recruiting, since it shows the range of new courses and concerns that a college will have to consider if it decides to recruit international students. While some will see international student recruitment as a revenue-enhancing measure, others will point out its educational value for local students. In either case, additional programs and services will be needed. These measures are reviewed by two veterans in this field.

Although these two chapters deal with bringing international students into the United States as a method of-enhancing the international flavor of a campus, chapters 4 and 5 take us into a new area, that of exporting local students to study overseas. It is certainly true that only a small percentage of community college students will ever be able to study abroad, but the number is growing. A college that is serious about providing a full range of opportunities for its students cannot neglect this area. Chapter 4 was written by Jody Dudderar from Rockland Community College in New York. Rockland is one of the leaders in developing and sending students to study overseas and is a founding member of the College Consortium for International Studies. Dudderar's chapter is a handy reference for anyone starting to develop either short-term or semester-length programs. Sometimes these overseas experiences also include a service learning or internship component. There is much interest in U.S. community colleges in service learning, and AACC has an active program in promoting it on the domestic level. Service learning abroad is even more rewarding, as Carolyn Kadel of Johnson County Community College tells us. In chapter 5, she reviews the various agencies with which colleges can cooperate in setting up these experiences and the steps that need to be taken if a college wants to do it on its own.

Chapters 6, 7, and 8 all deal with developing partners abroad. In chapter 6, John Halder, the president of Community Colleges for International Development, reviews several of the grant-funded projects of CCID members. Colleges interested in small-scale development work overseas will find that these projects provide faculty with a tremendous opportunity to become engaged in international activities. Most often these activities have some curriculum component connected to them, which eventually benefits all students. As this chapter points out, the availability of grant funds for this kind of work helps speed the process along and compensates colleges and faculty for their effort. In chapter 7, Frank Schorn shows how Austin Community College developed partners abroad to set up a system of exchanges geared toward the training of students interested in careers in high-tech fields. His chapter is drawn from his experiences with two U.S. Department of Education, Fund for the Improvement of Postsecondary Education (FIPSE) grants and can serve as a model for international cooperation between colleges, business, and industry in a variety of countries. While many community colleges might develop partners abroad without the use of outside funding, this chapter shows the range of activities possible through the FIPSE program.

The last chapter on partners is written by two veterans in international education from Florida, William Greene of Broward Community College and Robert Vitale of Miami-Dade Community College. Their chapter shows how, by establishing partners abroad, the U.S. community college can extend its reach through affiliates. Such partnerships provide not only financial benefit but also numerous opportunities for faculty development activities that carry over to the whole campus. It is worth noting that the affiliations discussed in this chapter were established without the help of outside funding.

Chapters 9 and 10 both show what can be done with curriculum development using grant money from federal sources. These chapters were produced by searching the records of the U.S. Department of Education for the most interesting and representative projects over the past few years. The projects selected are from business, liberal arts, and career programs. In chapter 9, Edward Stoessel of Eastern Iowa Community College discusses the results of four different projects in business education in India, South Africa, Ukraine, and Namibia. All four projects had local business as well as international partners. All dealt in some way with faculty and curriculum development, and all were federally funded. These projects are representative of what a small group of community colleges are doing in the business area. Others need to look at their local communities to see what connections might be expanded into an international partnership that will benefit the college and the community. Grant funds are not available for work in every country; but a number of developing countries come under the foreign aid umbrella of the United States in one way or another, and community colleges are prime candidates to take advantage of these opportunities.

Chapter 10, written by Fay Beauchamp of the Community College of Philadelphia, is representative of what is being done in liberal arts to infuse the curriculum with international content. In this chapter she argues that faculty development using an area-studies, interdisciplinary approach is a viable strategy for changing the curriculum and is an important source of intellectual stimulation for faculty. She bolsters her argument with many examples drawn from her own experience.

The last three chapters all deal with different topics. In chapter 11, Linda Korbel took on the job of collecting some of the less expensive ways in which colleges have internationalized their campuses. From displaying flags and wall maps to using international students as classroom resources, this chapter contains a number of ideas on how colleges can create an international/intercultural atmosphere on campus. Chapter 12 discusses the international activities of the American Association for Community Colleges. As Audree Chase explains, because of its location in Washington, D.C., and its acceptance as the voice for community colleges on the national level, AACC has done much to assist community colleges in the process of internationalization. She also provides a brief description of the leading organizations community colleges typically belong to, or work with, in their international efforts. The final chapter, by Allen Cissell and David Levin, outlines the sources of federal grants for community colleges in international education and helps us locate the Web sites where information can be found. The authors also offer tips on successful grant writing.

In the foreword to this book, Kent A. Farnsworth reflects on the events following September 11, 2001, and reminds us that teaching our students to "live outside the fence" is more important than ever. We hope that the chapters in this book will assist community colleges in that process.

Additional Challenges

Two areas, not explored thoroughly in this book, remain challenges for community colleges. The first is the role of foreign languages and the second is assessment.

Foreign languages have a weak foothold in the community college, being required, if at all, mainly in liberal arts transfer programs. Colleges that apply for the U.S. Department of Education Title VI-A grants, as chapter 10 illustrates, must include the development of foreign languages as part of their project. Most of the time, colleges propose to expand traditional language study or to add specialized instruction for career programs, such as Spanish for health science or criminal justice students. These short-term exposures to the language of the workplace are of some immediate practical value but lack the cultural component and the mastery of the language that would make the study of foreign languages a major contributor to the efforts to internationalize a student's program of study. It may be difficult to expand foreign language instruction at the community college level, but it is clear that we need to put more thought and innovation into this effort.

The second challenge is to include international education in our campus assessment efforts. The authors in this book would all claim that an increased emphasis on international/intercultural education will have the desired impact on students, but we have little evidence to prove it. Colleges must find ways of assessing this impact and include it in their learning outcomes and institutional effectiveness measures if they are to make a case for the continued funding of these efforts.

Acknowledgments

I am grateful to Donald A. Dellow for many suggestions and for encouraging me along the way; to Pat DeCoster for her typing and editorial assistance; to the people at the U.S. Department of Education in Washington, especially Sarah Beaton, Christine Corey, and Tanyelle Richardson for helping me select some of the grant projects to be included in this book; and to George Vaughan and his colleagues in the Department of Adult and Community College Education at North Carolina State University for inviting me to be a visiting professor in the spring of 2002. This invitation gave me the time to reflect and complete the final editing. And, finally, thanks to my wife, Ellen, who is my tireless supporter and chief grammar critic.

Bibliography

American Council on Education. 2000. *Internationalization of U.S. Higher Education: A Preliminary Status Report.* Washington, D.C.: American Council on Education.

Farnsworth, Kent A. 2001. "The Values of a Global Perspective." *Community College Journal* 68 (February/March): 8–14.

Levin, John S. 2001. *Globalizing the Community College.* New York: Palgrave.

.

CHAPTER 1

WHY DO COMMUNITY COLLEGES NEED TO BE INVOLVED IN INTERNATIONAL ACTIVITIES?

Donald A. Dellow
Broome Community College, New York

At the beginning of the 21st century, it is no longer necessary to say that the world is shrinking and that we are becoming far more interconnected than we have ever been. Everyone is aware of the greater competitiveness in the production and sale of goods and services; foreign interests own companies in our communities; greater numbers of our employees must travel to other countries as part of their jobs; U.S. stock markets rise and fall as foreign markets expand or contract. However, while almost everyone in America knows about these trends, it is safe to say that far fewer people have thought about the changes that must be made in our educational system if the United States is to maintain the level of global competitiveness it enjoys today.

Thankfully, a number of educational organizations have recognized the need for action. They understand that it will take a major effort to engage the academic community in change. A report by the American Council on Education stated that "unless today's students develop the competence to function effectively in a global environment, they are unlikely to succeed in the 21st century" (ACE 1995, 1). Another report coproduced by the American Council on International Intercultural Education (ACIIE) and the Stanley Foundation sounded a similar call to arms for community colleges to expand their efforts to produce a more globally competent citizenry:

> *To ensure the survival and well-being of our communities, it is imperative that community colleges develop a globally and multiculturally competent citizenry. (1995, preface)*

Both reports acknowledge the critical need for U.S. citizens to become more comfortable operating in other cultures. In addition, both acknowledge a concern that many in the United States have an isolationist attitude. There are still too many people who believe that U.S. dominance in world markets and world culture will ensure that other people will have to come to us and that we will not need to go to them. It is clear that those of us in higher education who have not begun to change our curricula to develop a more globally competent citizenry are tacitly supporting isolationism.

The tragic terrorist attacks on the United States could strengthen these isolationist tendencies. Some will say that the United States should pull out of multilateral organizations and that our invasive foreign policy brought about those attacks. Others will counter that this is not the time to retreat and concentrate on our own national interests. There is no national consensus on this issue, but it is certain what we as educators can do: We can encourage our students to enter this debate in a free and open way. In the forums held on our campus after September 11, 2001, there was a new interest in foreign policy and in learning about Middle Eastern and Arabic cultures, presenting us with an opportunity to build a more globally competent citizen who realizes that America cannot use its military power alone to protect its interests in an increasingly interdependent world.

What Is Global Competency?

The second report of ACIIE and the Stanley Foundation proposed the following definition of global competency:

> *Global competency exists when a learner is able to understand the inter-connectedness of peoples and systems, to have a general knowledge of history and world events, to accept and cope with the existence of different cultural values and attitudes and, indeed, to celebrate the richness and benefits of this diversity. (1997, 4)*

This is a good beginning in defining global competency, but the definition needs to be fleshed out more fully to focus on the actions that educators must play in the process.

In trying to understand what I, a community college president, needed to do to develop a strategy for preparing more globally competent students and workers, I found it helpful to envision a continuum of behavior that begins with personal awareness of cultural differences and culminates in a person successfully functioning in another culture or country (Figure 1.1). On this continuum I have tried to incorporate some of the ideas about global competency that were discussed in the two published ACIIE/Stanley Foundation reports (1995, 1997). There is obviously a much greater range of behaviors in the real world, but the essential point here is to describe global competence as increasingly complex behavior that ranges from awareness to behavioral proficiency.

Figure 1.1 A Continuum of Global Competency

Lower Levels of Global Competency

The left-hand side of the continuum would indicate the initial stages of global competency, where there is awareness of the considerable diversity in the United States and even more diversity around the globe. It is the first step in understanding that our way is not the only way.

Beneath each component of global competency on the continuum I have indicated the types of educational activities and experiences that would be minimally sufficient to promote the different levels of global competency. This helped me begin to understand what types of learning experiences and opportunities are necessary to develop greater levels of global competency in our students and in our community.

Again, the list of these activities and experiences is meant not to be exhaustive but rather representative of the increasing need for more immersion experiences if we are to reach the highest levels of global competency. Thus, under the awareness section of the continuum, the educational experiences necessary for development would be, at a minimum, the nurturing behavior of thoughtful parents, friends, and teachers.

The next point on the continuum is achieved when one attains greater knowledge of geography, politics, international events, and world economics. Many people seek out more information about these subjects once they become aware of their growing interdependence. This greater knowledge can be obtained through secondhand experience through the media or through formal education and self-study. General education courses in high school help provide a basic level of knowledge, and college courses that allow for more in-depth study and analysis are important in this stage of development. A trip abroad or a personal experience with an international visitor can intensify this thirst for more global knowledge.

The Internet, of course, has great potential as a tool in promoting interest in and access to global knowledge and cultural interaction. As Pulitzer Prize–winning author Thomas Friedman warns, however:

> *There is a danger that as a result of the Internetting of society . . . people will wake up one morning and realize that they don't interact with anyone except through a computer. (Friedman 2000, 474)*

Friedman writes persuasively about the need for that personal growth that comes from immersion in another culture or country. Certainly we have not evidenced the full usefulness of the Internet in promoting global competency, but it should not be perceived as the primary means of achieving global competency.

A person demonstrating greater cultural sensitivity in behavioral situations, most likely on his or her home turf, would illustrate the next step in global competence. A person who is able to handle interracial and intercultural exchanges in social or work situations would indicate competence at this level. At this point on the continuum more significant behavioral manifestations begin. Individuals are able to learn this sensitivity from direct experience with other cultures or groups. In an educational setting, this opportunity to learn may be enhanced by group work and simulation activities; media experiences alone are probably not enough to develop this cultural sensitivity. Having a rich exposure to members of other races and cultures on a campus, with thoughtful teachers shaping students' experiences, provides opportunities to develop greater levels of cultural sensitivity.

Higher Levels of Global Competency

The next two points along the continuum refer to successful interaction with people from other cultures or countries, at home and abroad. Experience leads me to believe that learning how to interact successfully with people from other cultures is easier when it is first done in the relative comfort of one's own country. Meeting international visitors and spending time with them would seem to be a necessity. International exchanges are an excellent way to provide these opportunities on campus and in our communities. One such program involving my local community brings groups of entrepreneurs from Russia and the former Soviet states to our campus for a two- or three-week period, during which visitors, students, and community members learn more about each other's culture, customs, and current events. Students who may never travel to Russia are given a wonderful opportunity to meet real Russians and to find out that their hopes and dreams are no different from their own.

The next step in the continuum assumes that a more demanding set of skills is needed to function effectively in another country or culture. Further differentiating, it is undoubtedly easier to develop global competence in a culture or country where language is not a barrier. Apparently, that is also what many current American study-abroad students think. According to an ACE report on the internationalization of higher education (2000), nearly one in four American study-abroad students chooses England, where the language is not a problem. Adjusting to a different culture, even one similar to one's own, can be challenging enough for many and can serve as the first step before going on to other study- or work-abroad experiences that require mastery of another language.

Traveling or studying in a country where a different language is required may be more challenging and stressful initially, but most people who do so report that the reward for their effort is a much better understanding of the culture than they would otherwise have. As language teachers have said for years, speaking the language makes all the difference.

Finally, the ability to live in another country and function successfully in social, educational, or work situations is a mark of the truly globally competent individual. This level of competence calls for traveling and living abroad for much longer periods of time. In my local community, a highly respected technology company has a German national as president, and he is also a leader in the community. He has an advantage over many other American CEOs in that he is able to communicate comfortably with colleagues around the world in several different languages. He is the epitome of the person who has the highest level of global competence. More Americans need to emulate him to function effectively around the world.

The Need for Greater Experience Abroad

In learning complex behaviors, the more successful experiences a person has, the greater the potential for mastery. It would seem that developing a comfort level in living and functioning abroad requires a major commitment to developing language proficiency and a major attempt to learn about the cultural differences of another society. For decades the European community has been encouraging its students to travel and participate in study-abroad programs or in work co-ops in other countries. The proximity of their countries and the policies of the European Union have promoted multilingualism and have therefore facilitated this transnational activity.

For the present, there is little expectation that all, or even most, community college students will study, live, or work abroad. But it is important to have more of them do so if they are to achieve higher levels of global competency and be better prepared for the future. The ACE report on the internationalization of higher education makes the point very clearly:

> *In the long run, those who can move seamlessly between different nations, cultures, and languages will be positioned to capitalize on the next scientific, technological, or information revolution. (ACE 2000, 30)*

The ACE report (2000), Friedman (2000), and Zachary (2000) all warn of the dangers of ethnocentrism, or the idea that good things will emerge only from American society. On the contrary, students who have experience in other countries bring back valuable ideas, insights, and perspectives that can help their country remain economically viable, to say nothing of other cultural perspectives that will enhance their own quality of life.

It is thus imperative to reflect on the educational experiences community colleges now provide and decide what can be done to promote higher levels of global competence. How many colleges have been able to offer international activities that assist faculty, students, and our communities in reaching these higher levels of competence? Isn't it time to talk about a comprehensive program of international activities that will allow more students to attain these levels?

Campus Leadership for Global Competency

The continuum of global competency in Figure 1.1 suggests that colleges must provide a variety of international activities if they hope to promote the kind of global competency students need. A comprehensive plan for internationalizing the campus would suggest the need to undertake curriculum reform; provide opportunities for international visitors on campus; offer study-abroad opportunities for students; and seek collaborative projects abroad for faculty, students, and other members of the local community.

In turn, it is difficult to undertake many of these activities without help from campus constituencies, the community, and other experienced professional colleagues. Other chapters in this book will detail some of the important resources available to assist those who are interested in providing additional opportunities to internationalize their campuses. My purpose here will be to make a special plea to the community college leadership.

For a college to completely embrace the vision of providing global competency, it is necessary that the highest levels of the college administration be committed to providing leadership for this activity. If the president is not out in front of this effort, the campus initiatives to build a comprehensive program of international activities will not get very far. The president needs to vigorously promote internationalism on campus, as well as to the trustees, local businesspersons, and other community leaders. Because the idea of international activities may not be received well in more provincial communities, however, the president needs to have in hand a well-thought-out plan to avoid possible risk to his or her career. In the aftermath of the tragic events of September 11, the challenge to provide leadership for international activities will be even greater.

Promoting the Need for Campus Involvement in International Activities

Because I had little international experience when I became a president, I drew heavily and frequently on the support of organizations like Community Colleges for International Development (CCID) and ACIIE to learn what I could. I had many opportunities to confront my own need to develop a greater global competence. Through my affiliation with those organizations and with other groups on campus and in the community interested in international education, I learned why community college involvement is so important. I also could draw on moral support in times of doubt and was given technical assistance when I was momentarily stalled. As part of my learning experience, I traveled with a group of community college colleagues on visits to colleges and universities in several other countries and thus learned firsthand how to develop both personal and professional international relationships.

Today, community colleges have a new ally and supporter in their efforts to encourage greater global competency. The Stanley Foundation has as one of its major missions the promotion of more global education in two-year colleges, and its state and national programs to promote greater global awareness have affected thousands of community college faculty, students, and laypersons. Their Web site, www.theglobalcommunitycollege.org, provides an excellent summary of strategies and activities for colleges seeking direction and guidance.

Sharing the Vision
Like any college president, I have many opportunities to speak to groups in the community. In doing so, I have usually provided three reasons for supporting a greater international involvement by our community college. The following themes seem to resonate well with these local groups.

I explain that our college is actively involved in international activities because we feel we must (1) respond to the demand for, and to the college's responsibility for, providing workers for our community who possess a more global perspective; (2) provide opportunities for students, faculty, staff, and the community at large to engage in personal foreign diplomacy to reduce provincial thinking, increase acceptance of diversity, and possibly add a little adventure to their lives; and (3) enhance revenue streams for the college and promote economic development in our community. It will come as no surprise to my fellow college presidents, however, that I do emphasize one reason more than another, depending on my audience. Let me say a bit more about each of these themes.

Preparing for Today's Job Market
The foremost reason for engaging a community college in a variety of international activities is to assist students in developing a more global perspective so that they become more effective employees. Business and industry today are desperately in need of persons who are able to function in situations of greater cultural diversity, at home and abroad. The workforce in the United States is becoming increasingly international, particularly in the healthcare and technical

fields. Employees who can work effectively in multicultural teams are becoming more and more valuable to their employers.

Zachary, in *The Global Me* (2000), argues persuasively that cultural diversity is a major asset in today's competitive global markets. He believes, and provides evidence to support his belief, that the strength of the U.S. economy comes in large measure from having a rich cultural diversity, borne of a constant replenishment of immigrants and refugees. He is convinced that the fuel of capitalism is a culturally diverse environment. Anecdotes throughout his book document the many benefits that accrue to those workers who have had experience with other countries and cultures. He suggests that a worker who has studied or worked abroad is better able to work cooperatively with the increasingly diverse workforce in his or her hometown. As Richard Stanley indicated in the first ACIIE/Stanley Foundation report, "If community college education has not equipped the student for this actuality, the student has been shortchanged and ill-prepared for the world in which he/she lives" (1995, 2).

Personal Diplomacy and a Sense of Adventure

The second major reason I give for our college involvement in international activities is that such an involvement provides opportunities for personal diplomacy and adventure. My college is fortunate to have programs that both bring international visitors to our campus and send our faculty and community members abroad on personal diplomacy and professional collaborative missions.

The programs that bring international visitors to my campus, such as the U.S. Department of State Community Connections Program and the Sister Cities Program, provide opportunities for hundreds of our students, faculty, and community members to learn firsthand about other cultures. Most of our international visitors stay at homes in our community for a period of several weeks, so they have the opportunity to share very personal cultural perspectives with students and the community.

A rewarding aspect of this kind of international activity is the excitement and enthusiasm it engenders. At the end of these international visits there is always a banquet featuring much celebration, personal sharing, and exchanging of gifts. Community partners who have been even marginally involved with our international visitors often express their great satisfaction at having been part of the exchange, which often promotes personal and professional relationships that continue long after the program has ended.

Another of our long-standing programs, funded by the Cooperative Association of States for Scholarships (CASS) program at Georgetown University, brings students from the Caribbean and Central America to my campus to obtain degrees in quality assurance and x-ray technology. Over the past 12 years, we have had 34 students each year who act as lay ambassadors, teaching us much about their countries and cultures. Their presence has encouraged many of our faculty and students to study Spanish. I have taken two different faculty groups to participating countries to visit our alumni, and alumni return to our community as friends and business associates.

Another type of personal diplomacy for the campus involves technical development and community collaboration activities. Both involve having teams travel to another country to assist an institution or a community in a mutually agreed-upon activity. In the area of technical development, our campus has had numerous grants to help foreign educational institutions understand and develop strategies to teach and support free-market economies. Invariably, our teams return with a greater knowledge of the country and a commitment to continue the relationships they have developed. Some of our faculty have engaged in several grant activities in Russia and have made more than 10 trips in connection with those grants. Our faculty and staff feel proud that not only are they reading about foreign diplomacy, they are also actively engaged in it.

It is also helpful to acknowledge that our technical assistance efforts promote U.S. economic interest. Since the U.S. economy depends upon an expanding world market for products and services, any activity that promotes greater understanding of and participation in the free market has the potential to benefit the U.S. economy.

International collaboration that involves local community groups is exceptionally useful in defining the college's international mission to the community. How better to do that than by working with a community group that promotes the exchange of citizens from other countries for the sheer enjoyment of promoting peace and world friendship? Community members and college employees have shared many trips in missions of personal diplomacy. These tend to build considerable support for the international activities of the college in the community.

Revenue Enhancement/Economic Development

Even the most conservative politicians or governance leaders will appreciate the economic benefits of having international students on college campuses and in the local community. In New York State, out-of-state students pay double tuition. They are also counted in the formula by which colleges receive state aid. In addition, international students bring with them money that pays faculty salaries, purchases local apartment rentals, and buys goods and services. For our college alone this amounts to a spending impact in the local community of nearly $2 million a year (2000), not considering multipliers.

As indicated earlier, campuses must have opportunities for native students to interact with and learn from those from other cultures. The international students who come to us provide just that kind of opportunity and confer the added value of helping our communities economically. For our local students who are a little more provincial in their thinking, the presence of international students in their classes offers a safe and supportive way for them to learn about other countries and their cultures. An international student organization on campus has been helpful in facilitating social interaction in which both the international students and our native students have an opportunity for more personal contact. We have found that friendships between our native students and our international students have sparked long-lasting relationships, culminating in travel abroad and, sometimes, even in marriage.

If colleges are to enjoy and benefit from an international student population, it is critical that they invest in support services like English-as-a-second-language (ESL) courses, international student advisers, and housing assistance. Success in providing these services will be rewarded by the word-of-mouth advertising from satisfied students who return to their native countries and comment on their satisfaction with their experience abroad.

Another way we have been able to enhance revenue for our college has been to participate in study-abroad consortia like the College Consortium for International Studies (CCIS). Consortium members handle the enrollments for individual programs (for example, our college is actively involved in the Italian and Dominican Republic programs), so all of the students enrolled from colleges across the country become Broome Community College students for that semester. This adds additional full-time equivalents to our funding base, resulting in additional income.

The revenue-enhancement and economic development benefits described above are among the least important reasons for increasing the international activities on our campuses. The revenue generated, however, can help support our efforts to develop additional international activities. Some colleges, in fact, use revenues from international activities to provide funding for faculty travel abroad and student scholarships for study abroad.

Success Breeds Success

As with most things, success with international activities tends to bring more opportunities for participation. When a college becomes known in the community as a place that has been successful in collaborating on international projects, people will seek it out when they have international projects. In addition, success in this arena begins to attract state-level and federal grant initiatives that require some previous experience with international projects.

More significantly, however, people on campus who have been involved with international projects tend to be more willing to seek opportunities and participate in them. Most of our federal and foundation grants that have funded international activity have been written by interested faculty members.

Conclusion

The AACC/ACCT report on the New Expeditions Initiative (2000) offered the following recommendation concerning globalism: "Community colleges should increase and expand programs for global understanding, including language and culture, that will help connect the various cultures in their own communities" (New Expeditions 2000, 8).

The international activities we have been able to develop at Broome Community College are easily within the grasp of any college where there is a commitment and a determination to promote a more global perspective for its students. Even with the number of international activities on my campus, it is still a struggle to ensure that the faculty, staff, and students make the most of them.

The mandate seems clear. To prepare students and communities for a future of greater global interconnectedness, colleges must develop a more global vision for their campuses. To do anything less shortchanges everyone.

Bibliography

American Association of Community Colleges and Association of Community College Trustees. 2000. *The Knowledge Net: A Report of the New Expeditions Initiative.* Washington, D.C.: Community College Press, American Association of Community Colleges.

American Council on Education. 1995. *Educating Americans for a World in Flux: Ten Ground Rules for Internationalizing Higher Education.* Washington, D.C.: American Council on Education.

———. 2000. *Internationalization of U.S. Higher Education: A Preliminary Status Report.* Washington, D.C.: American Council on Education.

American Council on International Intercultural Education and The Stanley Foundation. 1995. *Building the Global Community: The Next Step.* Conference report. Muscatine, Iowa: Stanley Foundation.

———.1997. *Educating for the Global Community: A Framework for Community Colleges.* Conference report. Muscatine, Iowa: Stanley Foundation

Friedman, Thomas. 2000. *The Lexus and the Olive Tree.* New York: Anchor Books.

Zachary, G. Pascal. 2000. *The Global Me.* New York: Public Affairs.

CHAPTER 2

INTERNATIONAL ENROLLMENT MANAGEMENT: ATTRACTING INTERNATIONAL STUDENTS TO THE COMMUNITY COLLEGE

Robert A. Frost
Parkland College, Illinois

To create a truly global campus, where students can study and learn to navigate the complex intercultural waterways of work, community life, home, and even church, community college leaders need to build the right global connections. Curriculum initiatives, study-abroad programs, global fairs, and college partnerships are all critical to this process. Perhaps the most difficult connection in creating this truly global learning environment is attracting international students to community college classrooms. We know that once they arrive, they tend to be model students, motivated and eager to form friendships with their classmates. We also know the economic benefits of attracting international students to our communities, as they will typically spend more than $20,000 per year for tuition, fees, and living expenses (Davis 2000).[1]

There are many factors involved in the recruitment and enrollment management of international students. Location, tuition and cost-of-living, quality of Web site, attractive academic programs, and a spirited marketing team are but a few of the essential ingredients this chapter will consider. For additional coverage of this topic, see the bibliography, which lists useful "hands-on" resource manuals.

During the early 1990s, international student recruitment was an activity low on the list of community college priorities. Less profitable than contract training and less exotic than faculty travel and exchanges, international recruitment was something colleges either contracted out or did not do at all. In addition to the perception that recruitment was a disreputable activity, there was little incentive from senior leaders and trustees to risk local funding for international endeavors. Of course, even to this day, state law or some college charters

---

1. The Institute of International Education (IIE) average is actually $30,500, but community college students spend from one-half to two-thirds that amount.

prohibit recruitment outside college-district boundaries. Fortunately for community college students, the pressures of funding, diversity initiatives, and other influences have combined to make international students a welcome addition to campuses today.[2]

Recently, community college international enrollments have been growing in double digits, and in fact account for most of the international student enrollment growth in the United States (Davis 2000). Community colleges have successfully identified their value to international students, developed marketing plans and advertising strategies, and opened their doors to the world. Perhaps most important, beyond tuition revenue gains and benefits to their local economies, college leaders today recognize that an international student presence is necessary for all college students to gain the global competencies required for career success. The first step in the long process of international enrollment management, then, is forming the service team to support this new and uniquely different population.

Campus Support for International Students

International students are a tremendous, and often forgotten, part of true campus diversity. There is great synergy in combining new, unique student populations with new staff and programming. Take advantage of this excitement in your recruitment by including a renewed commitment to service from all staff. Be sure to include (paid) student "ambassadors" who are part of the services team and remember that your best recruiters are satisfied students.

New staff can help new students become part of the community even while they are learning the details of their positions. So, although increases in staff and support can be tied to revenue and enrollment growth, the initial investment in support staff is critical (and necessary to the Immigration and Naturalization Service, or INS) to developing a solid reputation with your students, as well as with U.S. and foreign government agencies. Staff must remember the goal of helping students form strong bonds on campus so that these students see the campus as their home; a place to spend the entire day; a place where friendships and support are evident. Another way to look at this goal is to ask the question, "What can we do to encourage internationals to stay with us until they either complete the associate degree or meet their training objectives?"

---

2. In an October 2000 national videoconference on the topic of international student recruitment in community colleges sponsored by CCID, the Stanley Foundation, ACIIE, and AACC, many of the presentations by college leaders mirrored this sentiment. See the bibliography for information on the videoconference proceedings.

Finally, try to avoid losing staff who are successful recruiters. Much of international recruitment is really based on trusting relationships and when recruiters, parents, and even graduates overseas are making their recommendations to prospective students, they will often trust personal associations over institutional loyalties. As a result, it is all the more important to hire the right staff and support them, because if they leave, their recruiting contacts are more likely to follow them than remain with your college.

Laying the Groundwork

With any recruitment initiative, the board of trustees should approve of the concept and support the goals associated with increasing the international campus population. International recruitment entails some risks, so the board must be fully apprised of potential benefits and drawbacks, a best estimate of short-term and long-term costs, and the benefits expected within each time frame. Set up an evaluation framework with which international education staff can easily work, and inform the board that a campuswide service team of faculty and staff is committed to this effort. Above all, review the college mission statement with campus leaders and the board so that all agree these activities fall within the mission statement.

Service Team, Service Commitment

In one of the earliest complete works on international advising at community colleges, William O'Connell wrote that there should be at least one adviser for a population of 200 to 300 international students (1994). At Parkland College, the same people are involved in international admissions and advising, so closer monitoring takes place in matters ranging from immigration documents to emotional crises. Students can see these advisers for academic advising, travel documents, and community/housing information, and for information on any college service. Counselors can monitor cultural adaptation more effectively because they see students outside crisis situations.

Based on our experience at Parkland College, 1.5 advisers is a reasonable number to serve 300 international students, especially when responsibilities include admissions, matters connected with immigration, and academic advising and counseling (Kern-Brown 2001). Immigration regulations, the diversity of international students (visa students, immigrants, refugees, among others), and the limited family support system available to students all mean international advisers see students throughout the semester for many needs beyond the classroom and college.

Although advisers are probably the linchpin in the enrollment management chain, the real key is to assemble a dedicated team of faculty and staff to support their work. Faculty who enjoy spending time with international students, or who speak a foreign language, can lend great emotional support. Staff members who are willing to do the data entry for mailing lists, envelope stuffing, flier posting, and even outreach to local organizations such as churches, can play important roles in expanding recruitment efforts. Almost any college unit as well as the public relations/media department can take a lead role in a creative marketing campaign. These recruitment and service teams should meet regularly for two important reasons. First, mailing and similar advertising campaigns require brainstorming and advance planning. Second, international students, once on campus, need to be monitored and given the emotional support necessary to get over the initial cultural shock of academic life in the United States.

Emergency Response Group
It is never too early to plan for emergencies. One of the service tasks should be to form emergency response procedures for the particular challenges international students sometimes face. International students are vulnerable for many reasons: Many lack strong English skills, are living away from home for the first time, are accustomed to different traffic and other municipal regulations, and are often reluctant to seek medical, emotional, spiritual, or other types of assistance. It is only prudent to have an emergency response team in place composed of reliable faculty and staff who can assist students in times of crisis such as

- Being hospitalized and having no local family
- Being deeply depressed and lonely because of culture shock
- Being unable to return home when a death in the family occurs
- Having a medical, police, or similar emergency requiring interpreting or personal support services
- Experiencing a traumatic event such as a natural disaster or act of war
- Having a family emergency necessitating the need for an abrupt return home

The foreign student advisers may be aware of these situations, but they cannot cover all the issues, locations, languages, and expertise to meet all students' needs. Thus, a team of 5 to 10 people that provides this extra support can add tremendous depth to your college's international student support services.

Funding Recruitment
To effectively recruit international students, the college must establish a budget that recognizes the need to seek out students from a variety of sources. Local print ads, *Study in the U.S.A.*–type magazines, specialized Web sites, international

newspaper ads, and recruiting agents are but a few avenues that might be used. Selecting a strategy in each media outlet could cost more than $30,000, far more than even a midsize college can afford. Most schools (as workshop attendees report) start with budgets of about $15,000 for the first few years and then evaluate their results. It is best to avoid high-cost print/Web/online service combinations that promise to answer all your recruitment needs. Not only will you be competing with well-known "brands" like UCLA, but also today's students are learning how to shop around using the Internet and are less likely to rely on one service to locate the right school for them.

Perhaps the most important advice related to funding-recruitment initiatives is to plan and fund for the long term. Create incentives to reward the success of initial efforts (such as proportional increases in funding tied to enrollment growth) and allow gradual expansion of the program from local and regional efforts to global mailings and recruitment fairs overseas. Because recruitment affects funding, salaries, and classroom environment, consider how the college can best align available human resources with funding and other specific advantages (location, a university serving the area, immigrant community).

The Ingredients of Recruitment

Typically, a college with an English-as-a-second-language (ESL) program can attract international students

- From area universities and private ESL institutes who are seeking lower tuition costs, smaller class sizes, or entrance into college-level classes
- Through maintenance of a comprehensive Web site linked by keywords to all major search engines
- By focusing on five to seven expanding markets (e.g., Brazil, Indonesia, Thailand, Mexico, Republic of Korea)
- By advertising in a few solid, reliable markets such as Japan and Western Europe
- By mailings to high schools, advising centers, and ESL centers in countries likely to send students to the specific college and state
- By identifying countries or regions with close cultural, economic, or geographical similarities (e.g., Florida marketing to the Caribbean) and thus marketing the applicability of the study program
- By attending three to four overseas fairs in the same cities over a period of several years and thus furthering name recognition/ reputation

- If possible, through working selectively with a few trusted in-country agents or representatives. Today agents' fees are paid on a per-student or percentage basis, but be careful about agents who want to charge up to 25 percent of the student's tuition bill for each semester the student enrolls at your college. Students today transfer too often to make it worthwhile to pay more than a one-time fee.

How to Find and Exploit Recruitment Opportunities

Below is a quick recipe for getting started with international recruitment. You can flavor it according to your institution's needs, location, and budget.

- Join the four to five best-known international education organizations. This will automatically put you on the mailing lists of many service, recruiting fair, and similar organizations. You will also gain invaluable expertise from the conferences and workshops sponsored by these groups. For recruitment expertise and developing contacts with advisers and representatives overseas, try NAFSA: Association of International Educators. See chapter 12 for a list of other organizations.
- Approach the colleges, either in your region or elsewhere, who have private, independent intensive English programs (IEP) and who might be interested in a transfer program with your college. Your college added to their list of transfer schools can be a big plus to their reputation and recruiting goals. Your willingness to endorse their ESL program by accepting their graduates (usually students who have completed a specified level) results in your college receiving students who are eager to begin their studies. Even institutes in California appreciate relationships with midwestern colleges, as the California colleges are often only the arrival point for new students to the United States.
- Advertise locally and regionally as much as possible for the first few years. How many residents know your college has an ESL program, or that the college welcomes international students? Area residents will have friends working overseas, former classmates from college, and even family members who wish to study in the United States at reasonable cost. Consider forming a community task force that could function both in marketing and in seeking out residents with overseas contacts.

- Build a mailing list of the advising centers located overseas. These centers are the first stop for many prospective students. By sending a stock of brochures once or twice a year, your college is more likely to be promoted and to gain broader name recognition. Mailing addresses or labels can be located through the U.S. Department of State and other sites provided here (see Resources).
- Take advantage of the various government services and specialists working both in the United States and overseas. Perhaps the best example here is the Commercial Service of the U.S. Department of Commerce. Various services within this agency can alert colleges to recruiting fairs, help establish overseas contacts, set up meetings in-country, and advise on the marketing potential your college would have in a given region or country (see Resources).

Online and Other Distance Learning Partnerships

At Parkland College, all online courses for any out-of-district student are priced at less than half of the regular tuition charged to international students. Because Parkland College offers more than 100 online courses as well as online degrees, international students can save on room and board by completing as much of their degree as they prefer from their home country. Indeed, this new delivery system may yet prove to be the solution for the suspicious consular official who demands proof of a visa applicant's educational intentions—he or she will already be a student!

Not only are online programs cheaper to advertise, since much of their clientele will be searching online anyway, but also students will be much more strongly drawn to your campus if they know that their online hours will be included in their degree program.

There are many ways to strengthen this basic idea. For example, sign a joint degree program with a partner institution overseas that recognizes some transfer credit from the partner school's online courses but still requires that 15 to 32 credits be earned on your campus. Here, of course, the college gains the benefits of greater diversity on campus and builds the foundation for an expansive partnership. Another incentive idea would be to allow some ESL course work and the subsequent TOEFL score to substitute for foreign language credit. Such additions to online course work can encourage students to select your college over the growing list of online education providers.

Of course, there are a few negatives connected with online international education. First, the dropout rate can be even higher than the near 50 percent rate associated with domestic students today (Lewis 2001). Second, many colleges depend on ESL programs, Orientation 101, and similar introductory courses to generate revenue, given the often high out-of-state or international tuition rates. Online programs could depress on-campus enrollments initially, but overall enrollments are almost certain to go up over time. While much more research needs to be done on online instruction, clearly this medium is the way more and more students will be learning the virtues of a community college education.

International Partnerships

For many years, forming a partnership meant signing a sister college agreement that outlined activities the two (or more) colleges wished to complete together. Today, an overseas partner can serve as the U.S. college's representative and can even recruit in its country, or it can send only a few faculty each year for ESL training (while it seeks projects of joint interest with its U.S. counterpart). Perhaps the simplest partnership is one where the U.S. institution hosts 20 to 30 students in a three- to five-week ESL–American culture learning experience. Over several years (and 60 to 100 students later), your college will become a household name in the city of the partnership, and younger relatives and friends will follow in the program students' footsteps. Take this one step further: Why not offer to place $50 to $100 in a scholarship account for each student from the partner school who studies one month or longer? The funds can be built into program fees, will help to market your programs (one scholarship for every 15 to 20 students or partial scholarships for several in a program), and will build good relations with your partner institution.

Because educational partnerships are very common, historically, at the university level, be prepared for overseas counterparts to request equal exchanges (so no tuition is charged) for a small number of students each year.

While truly global, altruistic, and of great benefit in the long term, especially to the American students, such partnerships are not for colleges living within extremely tight budgets. For the bold or the true pioneers serving large campuses or districts, a few such partnerships can effectively link study-abroad, recruitment, and faculty professional development activities into long-term, mutually beneficial partnerships. Of course, linking the above also provides the glue that holds together all the components—including board support—we need to build the global campus.

Recruiting Is Marketing

In its most basic form, recruitment is advertising your college's "brand name," your model programs, and the various niches the college fills in the spectrum of educational programs. Stories abound of creative, catchy ideas that go far beyond the gift pencils students pick up at recruiting fairs. However, never discount the simple gift-pencil ideas either, as they endure for a reason. Here are some tips, with associated examples and ideas, to inspire some brainstorming among college marketing specialists:

- Get your name overseas. Consider offering to mail a T-shirt (and associated information about the college) to your student's younger sibling as a birthday present from your college. Expensive, yes, but look at the advantages: The student must provide you the address and can add a personal note and perhaps pay a nominal fee for the T-shirt, and the bookstore can run the program as a "good relations" campaign. By offering coupons or posting notices on campus, international students will learn of the "College Global Friendship Program." Of course, students can be allowed only a few mailings, and can be encouraged to send to those family members most likely to attend the college. An added benefit is that the bookstore buys into the collegewide recruitment team by offering a specialized service.
- All links eventually lead to your Web site. E-recruit services are fine because they will fill an important niche, but eventually a student needs to be impressed enough to apply online to your college. Make sure all services and ESL programs are linked and show a "wraparound" service commitment. Use lots of visuals, but make sure they work with all Web browser versions, especially older ones, with limited processing speed, as much of the world still operates on 100-megahertz processors. Try eliminating the fee for online applications or for students who apply in off-peak months. As with travel discount Web sites, these enticements can help prospective students follow through.
- Service alone is a marketing plus. Can you guarantee that your school can mail an I-20 within 24 hours? If not, it's time to process I-20s electronically with one of the several software packages now available. Can you ensure an airport pickup? Housing assistance? An emergency phone number? (Parents really appreciate this.) Services should be prominently displayed in a similar format or listing in all online and paper material.
- Local is global. Area churches, high schools, universities, migrant and refugee centers, municipal/sister city organizations, ethnic civic and social organizations, and professional immigrants are just some of the local means by which to attract international students to your campus. As Houston Community College indicated in a recent

Open Doors report, 76 percent of their 1998–99 international students reported that they came to Houston because a family member or friend lived there (Davis 2000, 16). Do not underestimate the strength of family ties, especially among non-Western cultures, as cost, support, safety, and common language are all powerful reasons students will often pick the place first, and then the college.

- Mix technology with low-tech advertising. As much as the Internet is the future, many people in the world cannot afford that future just yet. Advertising in magazines in select regions over a period of three to five years, mailing a few dozen brochures to each of the overseas advising centers associated with U.S. consulates and binational centers, and even local billboards can work. For example, Parkland College bought ad space in local public bus interiors for an entire year for under $1,000. In a town where thousands of internationals ride the bus to school and work every day, this was an exceptional value for the college's new ESL program.

- Market overseas. As stated above, annual mailings to advising centers are perhaps the least expensive way to advertise your programs globally. Once a database of the formal advising centers is constructed, you can begin to add the private ESL institutes, high schools, foreign embassy contacts, overseas industry partners, and other new contacts who will help distribute your materials. Of course, each college needs to decide which addresses to remove as well. This is where true expertise is necessary, as there are countries that send few students, and others that have long-standing cultural and educational ties to the United Kingdom or similar global competitors in education. Most important, there are far more locations around the world than colleges can afford to mail to, so the key is to learn from conferences and colleagues which nations, regions, and educational systems are likely to send the most students. The advising centers, while practically independent of the U.S. Department of State, often are housed in U.S. facilities or managed by U.S. nationals. While terribly overworked, these advisers do all they can to help prospective students come to the United States.

- Given the above, brochures must avoid "smorgasbord advertising," in which dozens of options and avenues to attain a degree are listed. While the U.S. educational system is partially based on choice, this can be confusing to non-natives. Show degrees and specializations, but avoid describing general education electives and the seemingly unlimited options of undergraduate education. Such details are better presented on a Web site that can show the many benefits of a community college education.

- Use personal contacts. When you travel overseas for any reason, make it a point to follow up with these front-line ambassadors for U.S. higher education. Take them to lunch if the timing is right. Establish contacts with the local ministry of education and U.S. trade officials. Try to set up an appointment in the visa section of the U.S. embassy or consulate where you are traveling. When visa officers know your college is serious about recruiting, and especially supporting, international students, your applicants are much more likely to be granted visas to study in the United States.

- Facilitate getting the F-1 student visa. Even though your college has accepted an international student and has sent an I-20 form indicating this, the prospective student still needs to apply for a student visa in order to enter the United States. While obtaining this visa may be indirectly related to marketing, educating your student and consular officials is a critical link to increasing your college's international enrollments. Your prospective students must understand the difficulties and responsibilities associated with applying to study in the United States.

- Your Web site and brochures should include such details as how to clarify educational goals before the consular interview (so the consular official understands why this person has selected a community college instead of an Ivy League school); the importance of showing funds on deposit in a local bank, or even a prepaid tuition receipt when completing the consular interview; and understanding the true purpose of the consular interview, which is to weed out illegal immigrants. In providing information to consular officials, remember that turnover in this job is high, and such letters, reports, and faxes pile up on consulate bulletin boards. Nevertheless, it is good practice to let the visa officers of a specific country know if you are planning a blizzard of marketing and recruitment activities in their region, and even ask their opinion on the likelihood of success.

What Do You Do If You Lack Location?

We all begin innocently believing that all international students would want to come to us, given the great things we know about our colleges. However, if you are recruiting from a small college, in a town without global name recognition, you probably realize your region is not a primary destination for international students. Statistics alone show most students will go to New York before they ever consider Kentucky, although this may change in light of the World Trade Center disaster.

Nearly half of all foreign students in the United States are enrolled at institutions located in merely 50 counties (Davis 2000). But chances are that equine science, forestry, mining technology, computer networking, and even engineering transfer students will want the specialized programs community colleges offer. The challenge, therefore, is to trumpet what we do best to the right audiences. Wastewater management, as well as numerous other specialized environmental programs, fire science technology, and precision agriculture are just a few examples of specialized programs sought by foreign national, provincial, and local governments.

At the same time that several unique programs are promoted, strengths related to the most popular fields, such as business, mathematics, communications, and even fine arts, should be emphasized. International students, as well as government officials involved in development programs, decide where to go for the very same reasons that motivate us: quality of education, low cost of living, safety within the community, availability of places of worship, stable economic base, and access to cultural and recreational activities. Proximity to a large city, and thus an international airport, should always be promoted. List any well-known universities with whom you maintain transfer agreements alongside the dollars saved by attending the community college first.

Those who work in a rural or remote college know a diverse international population is counted not in the hundreds but in the dozens. Obtaining international students can be done; but it requires seeking out the few specific students who really belong at your college. This involves the right mix of passive recruitment (mailing brochures and similar materials), active recruitment (recruiting fairs overseas, agents, agreements with ESL centers and cooperative universities), and an ongoing public relations effort by a spirited team of faculty and staff.

Passive Recruitment

Passive recruitment involves low-budget, limited efforts to attract international students. We know that 87 percent of all international students at community colleges are self-funded. By far, the majority of these students arrive to study within a few academic majors: The fields of business administration, engineering, and mathematics and computer sciences (reported as one area) account for nearly 46 percent of all international students in the United States. However, social and life sciences and fine arts together account for about 21 percent (Davis 2000, 15). While there may be more than 500,000 students studying in the United States, almost half of those students are graduate students. So, the community college challenge is to learn which markets, and which programs, will be the most attractive.

Community colleges should market the hands-on nature of their classrooms. Ads should show students training in an actual radio station or auto, computer, or hospital equipment repair center, or in other facilities related to their field. Since student access to such technology is rare in many countries, in color promotional literature, make ample use of photographs showing students actually manipulating the technology. Above all, in attracting students to your campus through passive means, including print ads, brochures, and a sizable Web presence, emphasize the outstanding academic advantages you have, but especially include examples of all costs.

Active Recruitment, or Working with Agents and Representatives

Recruitment by agents or representatives outside the United States must be done in an ethical and responsible manner. This includes their forwarding complete applications, English test reports, and such materials that allow the college to assess the representative's thoroughness in meeting prospective students' needs. Contracting recruitment to outside agents has become more accepted in the past four to five years.

There was a period in the late 1980s when NAFSA would not even endorse the practice of recruitment because of the numerous complaints that agents in other countries had misrepresented the colleges. Much has changed in the past decade, but community colleges still must be aware of INS regulations, the motivations of recruiters, and the many advantages of developing trusting relationships with the right agents.

Community college board members and senior administrators are likely to express concern over the high cost of working with outside recruiters. The way to resolve such concerns is through providing research that allows the college leadership to assess the benefits and costs for the given institution.

The Financial Side of International Student Enrollments

The benefits are clear and many; but what are the financial costs associated with enrolling international students? As part of our preparations for recruiting at Parkland College, we researched the tuition rates of more than 60 colleges across the country.[3] From this survey, we determined that the average cost for international

---

3. Through Web sites, brochures, and phone calls, we reviewed the tuition of the 40 community colleges enrolling the highest numbers of international students, according to *Open Doors*. Then we selected 20 similar midsize institutions from a group of midwestern colleges, including five other colleges in Illinois, where international tuition is high because of a state-mandated formula for determining out-of-district tuition rates.

students is about $147 per credit hour (Frost 2000). This figure will answer many questions your college probably has about recruitment of international students, about those already on your campus, and about whether the rate matches the quality of your institution. For example, it is unlikely that a college with tuition lower than this amount could cover instructional and service costs and pay any significant recruitment costs. In this case, many colleges implement an international student fee, an application fee, or work only with agents who themselves collect a standard fee from applicants (but such fees should be closely monitored, and should be connected to agent endorsements).

Thus, many community colleges today charge an application fee and then an additional semester service fee that is usually tied to the support services created exclusively for international students (and therefore would otherwise increase institutional costs). Colleges with higher out-of-state tuition rates tend to have fewer, if any, additional fees. Parkland, for example, has no special fees that international students must pay. While Parkland has no application fee, we have seen an increase in frivolous applications as well as in "hopeless" applications—applications from students who have no funds applying from countries in various states of economic or social upheaval, where it is likely the consular official will identify them as economic refugees and deny the visa application. These issues must all be brought into balance for a given college to attract students, maintain service levels, and yet not inundate staff with unproductive paperwork and data entry tasks. Perhaps best for all parties is to consider how all such costs can be totaled into a semester or annual package rate.

While at overseas fairs and meetings with foreign officials, I often longed for a flat rate I could quote to anyone asking about the cost of attending my college for one year. "Fifteen thousand dollars," I said once to a mother and father at the end of a long day of recruitment meetings in São Paulo, Brazil. But this only led to more questions. "Does that include housing? Meals? Books and fees?" When I answered yes, the next question was "And to whom, sir, shall we write the check?" This experience sums up much of good sales practice today: How simple can you make the transaction? Can you offer your client the product and services together in one package?

Related to such package fees is the concept of limiting tuition fees and partial tuition awards (similar to, but not exactly the same thing as, scholarships). Limiting tuition fees, practiced today by some state universities, involves charging students for up to 16 credit hours but allowing, for example, between 17 and 20 hours to be included at no extra charge. This provides an incentive for top students to come to your school, as they'll save more than a semester of tuition and living expenses over the course of a degree. Other advantages are obvious as well: The college gains a marketing edge; students will spend more time on campus and in classrooms; and students will be more likely to stay to complete the associate degree.

Retention is an important matter since international students are a mobile group. Colleges might consider advertising a tuition discount for the last semester before graduation. This provides some incentive to stay and the student views this as an award rather than a discount.

These are just a few ideas of many to consider that will help your college not only attract international students but also encourage them to stay until they complete their degrees.

Conclusion

Learning about international enrollment management is a little like studying the many tributaries of the Amazon River; it is a never-ending study of arrival points and departures, full of new discoveries. There are many ways for students to "flow" to our campuses, whether by their own paddling or by being carried on the torrents of political asylum.

We cannot even be sure what the students of tomorrow may bring! Equally so, there will always be new marketing ideas and better ways to serve our students. It is certain, however, that competition is increasing, both among community colleges and between two-year and four-year institutions. Such competition will eventually affect the tuition we charge, how we approach academic program evaluation, and, especially, our relations with overseas partners. The colleges that can maintain stable, meaningful, long-term relations with overseas partners have a great edge. Colleges with strong board support can initiate strategic initiatives that benefit all constituencies. In the end, international recruitment is a win-win endeavor, as it will enhance all aspects of a college's globalization efforts.

Bibliography

Althen, Gary. 1983. *The Handbook of Foreign Student Advising.* Yarmouth, Maine: Intercultural Press.

American Council on International Intercultural Education and The Stanley Foundation. 1995. *Building the Global Community: The Next Step.* Conference report. Muscatine, Iowa: Stanley Foundation.

———. 1997. *Educating for the Global Community: A Framework for Community Colleges.* Muscatine, Iowa: Stanley Foundation.

Davis, Todd M., ed. 1999. *Open Doors 1997/98: Report on International Educational Exchange.* New York: Institute of International Education.

————. 2000. *Open Doors 2000: Report on International Educational Exchange.*
New York: Institute of International Education.

Frost, Robert A. 1997. *Recruitment and Retention Report and Recommendations for Future Success.* Champaign, Ill.: Parkland College.

————. 2000. "International Student Management: Enrollment, Assessment, and Placement Methods and Services." Presentation at American Association of Community Colleges National Convention, April, Chicago.

Kern-Brown, Dede. 2001. Interview with R. Frost on Parkland College's international admissions and advising procedures, August, Champaign, Ill.

Lewis, Kathy. 2001. Interview with R. Frost on distance learning at Parkland College, September, Champaign, Ill.

NAFSA. 1992. *Standards and Policies in International Exchange: A Guidebook for Policy Development, Professional Conduct, and the Continuing Growth of International Education.* Washington, D.C.: NAFSA: Association of International Educators.

O'Connell, William. 1994. *Foreign Student Education at Two-Year Colleges: A Handbook for Administrators and Educators.* Washington, D.C.: NAFSA: Association of International Educators.

O'Hara, Marie, K. Raftus, and J. Stedman, eds. 2000. *NAFSA's Guide to International Student Recruitment.* Washington, D.C.: NAFSA: Association of International Educators.

Rosenberg, Seymour, ed. 1997. *U.S. Consular Posts Handbook.* 9th ed. Washington, D.C.: American Immigration Lawyers Association

Resources

Sites below include resource manuals, information on immigration law, and school and advising center addresses. Some of these may be used to develop mailing lists and recruiting ideas.

- American Immigration Lawyers Association (AILA). Publishes immigration-law publications serving the practicing immigration lawyer. Specific works on consular practices and visa processing, as well as consular post information, can be obtained from www.ailapubs.org.
- College Board. Unfortunately, the excellent *International Recruitment Kit* is out of print. The last edition is 1998. This kit was probably the one best source as it included disks with addresses in mailing label formats, the Directory of Overseas Schools (see above), and numerous perspectives on contacts, helpful sources,

and ways to meet the needs of international students. However, all these resources are now available through the other sites listed above. For more information, see the following Web sites:
www.collegeboard.org
www.collegeboard.org/ie/student/center/html/map.html
www.collegeboard.org/ie/html/admiss.html

- ISS Directory of Overseas Schools 2000–01. More than 540 abbreviated listings from the Directory of Overseas Schools are available on this Web site. This is a comprehensive guide to K-12 American and international schools located outside the United States. Depending upon the location and transfer programs at your college, top academic students overseas may find you through the counselors at these schools. Ordinarily, American students at these schools return to the United States to attend top-flight universities. However, many residents lack the funding to enter Ivy League schools but commonly have native English skills and still desire a U.S. education. See www.iss.edu/directory/directory.html. *Note:* Not practical for small rural colleges, but very valuable for targeting specific underrepresented countries and counselor contacts.

- NAFSA: Association of International Educators. Publications can be obtained from www.nafsa.org/content/ProfessionalEducationalResources/ Publications/publications/html.

- Parkland College, Champaign, Ill., Web site: www.parkland.cc.il.us

- U.S. Department of State. Provides limited support to a network of educational advising/information centers around the world. These centers advise prospective international students and other audiences on higher education and study opportunities in the United States. For more information, go to http://exchanges.state.gov/education/educationusa.

CHAPTER 3

DEVELOPING ENGLISH-AS-A-SECOND-LANGUAGE PROGRAMS AND STUDENT SERVICES

Scott Branks del Llano, Richland College, Texas
Jeana Remington, Dallas County Community College District, Texas

This chapter will present a framework for developing English-language learning models and offering a full range of services to support international students coming to the community colleges in the United States. It will also discuss ways to integrate these students into the college academic curriculum, provide them with intercultural communication skills and cultural adjustment assistance, and encourage a wide range of experiences that bring a whole, well-rounded interchange during their time of study and personal growth. The models discussed here emerge from two philosophical frameworks. One is the principle of learner-centered curriculum development, and the second is a holistic human approach to hospitality and support services. A crucial element in creating language-acquisition education is to honor diversity through a variety of student learning options and a broad range of services that are sensitive to the many teaching and learning styles and cultural differences in the population served. While much of what we will have to say applies to the immigrant student population that community colleges serve, our primary focus is on the international (visa) student population.

A Curriculum Delivery Model
Language Instruction
Working in an innovative, student-centered environment, such as that found in most community colleges in the United States, fosters the continual search for new and improved programs and services to our communities. In a world that daily becomes smaller while our communities become more global, the answer to the age-old question "Who is my neighbor?" continues to expand. As a college seeks to bring about interactions that respond to expressed needs in an international environment, it might ask itself "Who, What, Why, and How" to plot its course.

A responsive institution must scan the environment in which it operates. The institution needs to ask, "Who needs or wants services?" The current situation in community colleges shows a dramatic rise in the request for international student programs and services. For example, Richland Community College in Dallas, Texas, is located in the center of a fast-growing international community made up of lifelong Texas residents, long-term immigrants, new immigrants, and nonimmigrant international workers.

To initiate the environmental scanning process, our institution charged a task force composed of faculty and staff with designing a comprehensive English-as-a-second language (ESL) curriculum. The initial study group surveyed exemplary ESL programs across the United States and adapted elements of the programs to a series of courses that could suit the varying requirements of a multicultural/multilingual population. The model that arose from this work views the acquisition of a second language as a developmental—but not a remedial—process. Offering four separate courses in reading, writing, grammar, and oral/aural communications at four proficiency levels provides both flexibility in scheduling and recognition that in specific individuals, proficiency levels may vary from one skill or content area to another.

Designed to accommodate the geographic, numeric, linguistic, and cultural diversity experienced by seven campuses scattered across a large urban county, the model allows each campus to transform its program with maximum consideration for students' needs and preferences.

The Basic Curriculum Model

The basic model grew out of the developmental reading and writing curriculum of the colleges. The first ESL courses were special remedial sections targeted to non-native speakers of English. As the numbers of students in such sections multiplied, the need for a focused curriculum emerged. Providing courses in the areas of oral/aural communications, reading, writing, and grammar, the ESL curriculum is designed to address the academic language needs of non-native English speakers from advanced-beginner through advanced levels. Courses are taught in a semester time frame as three-credit-hour courses. Students receive nontransferable, institutional credit for the completion of each of four courses at each of four levels.

At Richland College, where the enrollments of ESL students grew from 25 in 1986 to more than 3,000 in 2001, the basic model served well, while the college's burgeoning international population, along with its sincere interest in internationalizing the total college curriculum, brought a variety of additional needs to light.

With the continuing growth of the non-native English-speaking population in the Dallas area, the demand for diverse programs to meet not only academic preparation requirements but also workforce and social needs gave rise to the development of a noncredit workforce development ESL curriculum. Workforce ESL courses are offered through the continuing education program and provide seven levels of instruction. Students are assessed and registered for the program but are not required to fulfill the college admission process. The courses consist of 60 hours of instruction per level, with additional courses available in accent reduction, business English, technical writing, and TOEFL preparation. Curriculum is updated through periodic review by teams of noncredit ESL instructors—administrative personnel acting in consultation with credit ESL instructors—to allow for a smooth transition from noncredit to credit programs. Attention to community demand and care for the quality of the curriculum in all programs spawns continuing growth in ESL programs.

The "Who" Question

The continuing demand for ESL services reveals that services to international students are, indeed, services to the local community. In answering the question "Who," the college began to look at the continuing flood of requests from foreign students for admission to the college, both for college-level programs and for English language instruction.

Frequently, the primary concern of the international student is to pursue college-level or graduate-level university study with English language acquisition a distinctly secondary consideration. Therefore, from the student's perspective, English language instruction should occur in a format that provides for the swiftest reasonable completion.

Recognizing that students to be served in an English-for-international-students model will generally be well educated and highly literate in their first languages, the model views the acquisition of a second language as a developmental—but not necessarily remedial—process. Helping students transfer learning skills and academic strategies from the first to the second language must be included in the preparation of curriculum. Additionally, students attending U.S. institutions on student visas or in student status have different life situations from many of their U.S. immigrant counterparts in that visa students are presumed to be studying full time rather than studying to augment their current full-time occupation in the U.S. workforce. Finally, achieving academic competence must include not only proficient language use but also the skill to function appropriately and effectively in the higher education system. Teaching effective intercultural communication plays a significant role in any ESL program. Later, this chapter will take up the intercultural communication component of the curriculum. Deliberating these questions and observing how other institutions address them will lead the program development team to form a vision for an instructional program that prepares students for academic success in U.S. higher education.

The "Why" and "How" Questions

Vision takes on substance as designers begin to formulate an answer to the question "Why should we deliver the requested services?" Alice Chandler writes, "Both altruism and self-interest demand 'global stewardship'—a recognition of the interconnectedness of nations, of the need to narrow the gap between 'have' and 'have not' nations, and of the worldwide obligation to address global problems of health, population, and environment. Foreign trade and foreign policy are no longer elitist domains. They are the necessary and proper concerns of an informed citizenry and an integral requirement for America's educational system" (2000). Inviting both immigrant and nonimmigrant students to the community college campus is an essential action in preparing not only local students but also those students who honor us by accepting our invitation to participate in an ever-shrinking global environment.

Having contemplated and answered questions regarding needs and motivation, we can move forward to elaborating an instructional model that is sensitive to the environment in which it will exist and is congruent with the values of the institution. "How shall we deliver the programs and services demanded by this population?" The model developed for Richland College is framed in an intensive, fast-track delivery model. Providing classes in eight-week sessions consisting of 25 hours of instruction per week permits students to complete as many as five semesters of course work within an academic year plus one summer session. (Admittedly, only the ablest and most dedicated of students proceed from the first through the fifth level in this period of time. However, the average student enters the program at an intermediate to high-intermediate proficiency level and thus is able to complete the entire program in one to one and one-half semesters.) The development of the remaining curriculum features, then, occurred in the context of a fast-track, intensive English program.

The intriguing outcomes of the learning-communities model advanced by Evergreen State College in Washington form a philosophical base for the instructional model. In addition, the principles of instruction for academic and communicative competence, as well as professional experience, seem to point to the need to place skills and content instruction in an integrated environment. Therefore, courses in the program are integrated and thematic. In other words, while students receive grades in reading, writing, grammar, and oral/aural communications, their instructional day is seamless, as all content and skills taught are entwined with the materials and experiences designed by the instructors.

Even so, specific instruction in each skill area takes place as needed. It is expected that principles of language use are reinforced throughout the curriculum—reading skills may be revisited as the class works on a writing-focused activity; listening/speaking skills are reinforced during class discussion of reading assignments. Course themes related to understanding and addressing social problems or understanding oneself in order to understand others serve to unify the curriculum. They also provide time on the task of working through extended projects in reading, writing, research skills, and communication proficiency. Such cohesion in the delivery of ESL instruction seems to provide students with greater fluency not only in communication skills but also in the processes of U.S.-style higher education.

The program focuses on the development of academic English language skills. Because it exists in an environment that places high value on written communication skills—indeed, that judges not only the quality of the graduate but also the quality of the institution on such skills—the program tends to be weighted toward writing instruction. While writing skills are strenuously evaluated, exit criteria have been developed for all skill areas. Students must demonstrate mastery of all skill areas before being promoted to the next level of instruction. Mastery is demonstrated by successful attainment of exit competencies and achievement of an average grade of 80 percent across all courses.

The ongoing assessment and evaluation of student progress begins with the student's initial application. Every student entering the program is assessed locally (whether or not a TOEFL score has been presented). All new students are required to sit for an in-house-administered placement test in reading, grammar, and vocabulary. Following the objective assessment test, a writing sample is administered. Writing topics are presented based on the objective test scores. Students scoring less than 20 percent on the test are retested with a basic grammar skills test. Students scoring in the advanced-beginner to intermediate range of the test receive narrative or descriptive topics. Students scoring in the high-intermediate to advanced range are given persuasive or argumentative topics. Ongoing assessment involves classroom testing and measurement against program exit criteria. Thus, through a comprehensive curriculum supported by clear placement and progress measurements, the program strives to help students achieve their goal of academic proficiency in English for college- and graduate-level study. And, perhaps the most important evaluation of all concludes each session as students are asked to evaluate their educational experience in the intensive English program.

The ideal ESL program is difficult to identify, and to propose a specific model as a standard by which to measure all others would be a topic for hot debate. The elusive ideal program is elusive because communities in which such programs are formed are unique. Their needs as well as their resources vary greatly. However, an ideal ESL program should have one characteristic: an unflagging desire to understand its population, to serve its students well, and to innovate gently but constantly.

Incorporating International Students into the Academic Mainstream
To maintain a program that supports international students, a community college must provide more than language instruction. Even a comprehensive curriculum with adequate assessment systems will not necessarily prepare international students for maximum success in their academic endeavors. To fully discharge our responsibility to provide students with the needed foundation for additional study, we education providers must be aware of the demands that undergraduate- and graduate-level students face and provide courses and experiences that facilitate the student's experiences.

To this end, it was necessary to continue asking the "Who, What, and How" questions by consulting with the receiving college-level instructors in English composition, speech communications, U.S. history, U.S. government, and mathematics courses. At Richland College this consultation led to the development of the "Bridge Program." The program uses freshman general education courses in a sheltered environment to polish the student's college-level reading, writing, and oral/aural communication skills. Two 3-credit-hour courses are taught in a fast-track semester of eight weeks. Since these courses serve multiple purposes, the selection of two courses that are desirable for most degree programs was a primary consideration.

Certain general education courses are typically required for a bachelor's degree from a public institution of higher education. Examples of such courses in Texas are English composition, Texas and U.S. government, American history, and mathematics. Additionally, Texas students must pass a state-mandated examination that has sections on writing, reading, and mathematics. Typically, international students pass the reading and math sections early in their U.S. academic careers. However, the writing section often proves to be a solid barrier for non-native writers. Therefore, one of the courses chosen for the Bridge Program was freshman-level English composition. This course helps students meet the testing requirement while crossing into the mainstream curriculum and achieving their first U.S. college-level credits.

The second course selected for the Bridge Program was the first semester of U.S. history. While students often develop adequate reading skills to accurately interpret college-level texts, they are frequently unprepared for the volume of reading required for studying college-level materials. Using the U.S. history course as a vehicle serves to continue the students' culture learning while they are initiated into the faster study pace of college-level courses.

While content is important, methods of delivering instruction are instrumental in facilitating student success. Course instructors are chosen for their experience with diverse student populations and their interest in using teaching techniques that are suitable for second-language learners. Such techniques may include exercises that precede the actual reading, such as developing vocabulary lists and outlining chapters. Strategies such as testing over smaller units of material at more frequent intervals provide support for the international student while ensuring that academic standards are upheld.

While the institution continually works to improve its systems and programs, initial research data collected by the college indicate that 70 percent of students who complete the intensive English curriculum achieve grades of A, B, or C in their college-level courses. At the same time, native speakers of English who are assessed into the college program at the college level achieve grades of A, B, or C at a rate of approximately 55 percent. In other words, students with intensive ESL instruction made a higher percentage of A, B, or C grades in college-level courses compared with their peers. Incidentally, withdrawal rates in college-level courses were significantly lower for this population as well. Thus, a model based on meeting the assessed needs of the targeted group that achieves its goals in a meaningful way can result in a program that provides increasing degrees of success for international students.

Intercultural Education

Any dynamic language learning program will enhance international students' understanding and skill in effective intercultural communication and behavior. Introducing students to the culture and richly diverse heritage of the United States is also a crucial ingredient to their success as they journey as guests within the host country. Further developing intercultural competence among students from diverse backgrounds through interactive experiences can provide a rich and thriving resource for your campus and community.

There are many reasons for including culture studies and intercultural communication in a language program. First of all, students will gain awareness of how their own culture has shaped their identity and worldview. This leads to their deeper understanding of certain behaviors within a culture and helps them construct a framework for identifying their own cultural patterns, as well as integrating aspects of the new cultures with which they interact daily. Understanding cultural differences can also be applied to increasing awareness of learning and communication styles as well as offering interesting context and life situations through which to learn relevant language.

When creating a culture component within the curriculum, colleges should define *culture* and build the curriculum on sound research in the stages of intercultural development. Sheila Ramsey defines *culture* as "a frame of reference consisting of learned patterns of behavior, values, assumptions, and meaning, which are shared to varying degrees of interest, importance, and awareness with members of a group; culture is the story of reality that individuals and groups value and accept as a guide for their lives" (1996, 1).

Culture is often divided into two categories. One is *objective culture,* which looks at the institutions of a culture, such as its art, literature, drama, food, and music. The social, economic, political, and linguistic systems may also be included in objective culture. The other is *subjective culture,* which refers to the less obvious aspects of a culture. Subjective culture deals with the psychological thinking and behaviors that define a particular group of people. "A good working definition of subjective culture is the learned and shared patterns of belief, behaviors, and values of groups of interacting people. Understanding subjective culture—one's own and others'—is more likely to lead to intercultural competence" (Bennett 1998, 2).

A comprehensive culture curriculum should examine both aspects of culture. The activities should encourage discussion of both explicit and implicit culture, but they should emphasize subjective culture and ways to explore the underlying values and patterns of culture. Students should be encouraged to experience the manifestations of these cultural patterns through the art, music, theater, media, community events, and other institutions of the host culture.

The content of a culture curriculum should move from the general culture approach, exploring what is common to most cultures, to a more culture-specific focus in the final stages or levels of the program, where students look more deeply into the facets of U.S. or American culture. The general culture foundation provides, throughout the course, an understanding of the general cultural variability factors that influence communication between people from different cultures and ethnic groups. This, in turn, provides a frame for interpreting the culture-specific information students will experience both in class and in their day-to-day interactions (Gudykunst et al. 1995, 3). Such a program must respond to the patterns and progressive stages of culture shock and also follow existing models for the stages of intercultural sensitivity.

Course content will hence begin with a focus on the ethnocentric states of development, which include denial of difference, defense against difference, and minimization of difference. As students move into a deeper understanding of cultural variability and the differences in behavior and value that result, the course activities should progress to reflect ethnorelative states of acceptance, adaptation, and integration of differences at the same time that the focus becomes increasingly culture specific to the host culture.

Another effective way to create a climate of cultural understanding and openness to diversity is to educate faculty and staff in intercultural competence. At Richland College, a core segment of professional development requirements focuses on assisting employees through the stages of intercultural development in a series of workshops. This series begins with the recognition of differences and moves through the various developmental stages, ending with the application of knowledge to achieve empathy and the understanding of multicultural frames and the final stage of encouraging the integration of differences. As faculty and staff are introduced to this process, a current is created in the educational environment that embraces differences and celebrates the gift of diversity granted by a truly international community.

Student Support Services

The admission of F-1, international, and ESL students carries with it an ethical responsibility to provide a full range of student services consistent with the unique needs of this special population. The comprehensive student services and resources discussed in this chapter are recommended in compliance with the federal regulations of the Immigration and Naturalization Service (INS) as well as the code of ethics established through NAFSA: Association of International Educators (1992). While detailed descriptions for each service cannot be presented here, there are a number of books and volumes that provide thorough procedures and resources for student support services. The bibliography lists a few of those publications. The following is an overview of the scope and nature of the services institutions should try to provide for their international student population, with a focus on the needs of F-1 visiting international students.

Predeparture and Orientation

It is essential for visiting students to have detailed knowledge of all requirements and information regarding the environment they are about to enter. Preparing students in advance can alleviate many of the cultural and adjustment challenges they will face. Many countries have an overseas adviser or U.S. educational advising center in the capital city; many are hosted through the U.S. embassy. Students should be encouraged to visit with an adviser in their country prior to travel. Another effective way to prepare students is to mail an information packet to the students once they have been accepted to your institution. Students need accurate assessments of their financial obligations both for tuition and for all living expenses. They also need accurate information on dates and immigration documents and processes, as well as travel tips. Their transportation and housing situations should be confirmed before they arrive.

Arrival and Orientation

Welcoming international students at your institution is crucial to shaping their positive first impressions and smooth adjustment. It is easy to overlook some of the anxiety in first-time students, particularly when they appear confident and capable. Students from many cultures may not be accustomed to asking for help, so it becomes an even greater responsibility to provide thorough information for students through an orientation program upon arrival. It is important not to assume that students know the cultural "rules" and climate of their host environment. Something as simple as jaywalking may result in undue stress for a student. As another example, many students come from countries with socialized medicine and are not aware of the exorbitant costs of healthcare in the United States. It is crucial to offer students a comprehensive medical insurance plan approved by international education organizations such as NAFSA to guarantee that students' health needs are met, including medical evacuation and repatriation. Creating a diverse advisory team composed of representatives from the many offices on campus as well as community members may help ensure that all aspects of academic life and community survival are incorporated.

International Student Office

Institutions serving F-1 students must have a location on campus dedicated to international students and staffed by trained professional foreign student advisers. These advisers facilitate all procedures in compliance with immigration laws and regulations and are aware of the ethical responsibilities involved in the enrollment of international students. Students need to know they have an advocate and mentor to whom they may come with any concern. The international student office serves to indicate an institutional commitment to educating foreign students and serving their diverse needs. Students must have access to quality academic advising as well as guidance in the planning of their degree and career paths. This service should continue from their initial assessment and placement all the way through the completion of their degree plan or transfer status.

Personal Advising, Counseling, and Survival Skills

If students are to feel free to ask questions, express concerns, and acquire the assistance they need as they continue their studies, personal advising and counseling must be accessible to them. This may be housed in the international student office or through referral to partner offices on campus. Students will often encounter difficulties or questions once they are well into their program; hence the orientation and personal assistance must follow them through their entire stay. One other helpful resource is to create a student handbook that contains all of the information needed, including a list of individuals and centers on campus and in the community that offer support.

Student Support Services

International students should be guaranteed full access to all student support services on campus. It may be helpful to conduct a complete tour of the facilities and introduce students to the key individuals who may assist them when they need support. In addition to the standard support services, students may also want to participate in such programs as conversation partners, tutoring, buddy systems, mentors, or other activities that partner them with U.S. students and community members.

Communication—Home and Here

Part of any adjustment to a new environment is the ability to connect with what is familiar. Students should be able to communicate with home and have full access to community resources. Particularly in incidents of crisis, war, or emergency, international visitors must be familiar with communication options. Services should include student e-mail and Internet, long-distance access, local culture-specific organizations, churches and places of worship, and chambers of commerce.

Social Activities, Sports and Recreation, Clubs and Connections

Academic life is not the only life students should experience. A well-rounded program should introduce students to social activities, student clubs, and community events that stimulate interpersonal relationships and meet emotional needs. It is also crucial to integrate these students into college activities and community life, as they bring a rich cultural diversity to these events.

Safety and Security

Guaranteeing student safety and security is increasingly important. Institutions must have clear procedures and communication systems in place to assist students in the event of an emergency, health risk, personal assault, or injury. Students need to feel they are in a safe environment and know what steps to take if they feel they are at risk. As recent events suggest, special consideration must be given to the protection of students who may feel threatened by world political events. In addition, educating students regarding sexual harassment and simple steps such as knowing how to dial 911 in emergencies is vital to their well-being.

Family Issues
If students are traveling with family members, they will need additional information regarding issues such as childcare, school systems, medical insurance for dependents, visa regulations, and other needs.

Community Contacts and Resources
Creating a network of community organizations and partners can provide support to international students that college staff simply do not have the time to give—for example, evening or weekend activity or assistance. Some suggestions for partners in this network include local businesses, cultural centers and chambers of commerce, rotary clubs, community events organizations, legal organizations, public services, healthcare organizations, places of worship, and other international organizations.

Reentry Orientation and Future Plans
Whether students are continuing their education in the United States or returning home, it is critical to prepare them for what lies ahead. They will be experiencing more adjustments and entering yet another new environment. Encouraging students to build a network of support, draw on their education and experience, and stay connected with those who have supported them thus far can greatly assist their transition. Offering workshops on reverse culture shock and reentry issues is an essential component to their success and ability to take full advantage of their education.

Conclusion
International students bring rich cultural diversity and world perspective to our campuses. They also bring unique challenges and expectations that must be incorporated into the strategic planning and learning programs of community colleges. Higher education faculty and staff would do well to practice hospitality and education that take a holistic approach to fully meeting the goals and expectations of students in both their academic and social lives. The more institutions are able to bring students together in successful and life-transforming ways, the more closely our world can move toward the global interconnectedness and peaceful understanding between nations that are so vital to the survival of the human race.

Bibliography

Adamson, H. D. 1993. *Academic Competence: Theory and Classroom Practice: Preparing ESL Students for Content Courses.* White Plains, N.Y.: Longman Publishing Group.

Bennett, Milton J. 1998. *Basic Concepts of Intercultural Communication: Selected Readings.* Yarmouth, Maine: Intercultural Press.

Branks del Llano, Scott. 1998. *The International Community College: Developing Comprehensive Programs at Two-Year Institutions.* Washington, D.C.: NAFSA: Association of International Educators.

Chandler, Alice. 2000. *Paying the Bill for International Education: Programs, Partners and Possibilities at the Millennium.* New York: NAFSA: Association of International Educators.

Gudykunst, W. B., S. Ting-Toomey, S. Sudweeks, and L. Stewart. 1995. *Building Bridges: Interpersonal Skills for a Changing World.* Boston: Houghton Mifflin.

Kendon, Gudrun. 1994. *Crossing Cultures: A Manual for an Extended Orientation Program for International Students.* Working Paper no. 46. Washington, D.C.: NAFSA: Association of International Educators.

Lustig, Myron W., and Jolene Koester. 1996. *Intercultural Competence: Interpersonal Communication Across Cultures.* 2d ed. New York: Harper Collins.

Meucci, Louis M. 1995. *The Dynamics of Diversity: Exploring Issues of Diversity on Campus and in the Community.* NAFSA Working Paper no. 53. Washington, D.C.: NAFSA: Association of International Educators.

NAFSA. 1992. *The NAFSA Ethics Program: Ethical Practice in International Educational Exchange.* Washington, D.C.: NAFSA: Association of International Educators.

———. 1996. *International Student Handbook.* 1996. Washington, D.C.: NAFSA: Association of International Educators.

Nunan, David. 1993. *The Learner-Centred Curriculum.* Glasgow: Cambridge University Press.

O'Connell, William. 1994. *Foreign Student Education at Two-Year Colleges: A Handbook for Administrators and Educators.* New York: NAFSA: Association of International Educators.

Ramsey, Sheila. 1996. "Creating a Context: Methodologies in Intercultural Teaching and Training." *Experiential Activities for Intercultural Learning.* H. Ned Seelye, ed. Yarmouth, Maine: Intercultural Press.

Reid, Joy M., ed. 1998. *Understanding Learning Styles in the Second Language Classroom.* Upper Saddle River, N.J.: Prentice Hall Regents.

Storti, Craig. 1999. *Figuring Foreigners Out: A Practical Guide.* Yarmouth, Maine: Intercultural Press.

CHAPTER 4

DEVELOPING AND ADMINISTERING STUDY-ABROAD PROGRAMS

Jody Dudderar
Rockland Community College, New York

The surest way to give students a global perspective is to provide them with an opportunity to live and study in another country. Many returning students report that this was the single most important experience in their lives. Largely for this reason, study abroad has gained wide acceptance in the United States as a valuable educational opportunity.

For many years, the junior-year-abroad model was the sole route to this kind of experience. Today, U.S. college and university students can choose from an array of options. With the democratization of higher education over the last 40 years, the participation of undergraduate students of all ages from a wide range of institutions has been increasing. Since these statistics were first compiled by the Institute for International Education (IIE) in 1986, the number of U.S. students participating in academic programs overseas has grown considerably. The largest gains have taken place in recent years, with enrollment leaping by 13.9 percent in 1998–99 to 129,770 U.S. students abroad. The increase in enrollment is accompanied by an expanding number of programs abroad; a greater racial, ethnic, and gender diversity of participants; a greater range of academic disciplines offered abroad; and an expansion in the number and type of institutions actively encouraging their students to study abroad (Davis 2000).

Community colleges have played a small but increasing role in this expansion. In a 1996 survey conducted by the American Association of Community Colleges (AACC), 35 percent of the responding community colleges supported study-abroad opportunities for their students (Chase and Mahoney 1996). By 2000, this number jumped to 60 percent, according to the AACC's follow-up survey (Blair, Phinney, and Phillippe 2001).

The value of study abroad to an individual's education is viewed variously as enriching the overall academic experience, augmenting multicultural development, promoting personal and intellectual development, increasing foreign language proficiency, and developing an international perspective (Kauffmann et al. 1992, Laubscher 1994). These benefits directly affect the student participant, but the value added to the institution can also be significant. The campus environment is affected by the influence in the classroom and on cocurricular activities when students return from abroad. These students will enliven class discussions with their fresh worldview and will bring new possibilities for campus activities based on their experience in their host country. In addition, the professional development of the faculty is supported through their involvement in creating and monitoring study-abroad programs, and the curriculum is enhanced through efforts to integrate these overseas academic activities into the fabric of the institution.

Getting Community College Students to Study Abroad

While few colleges would explicitly discourage their students from pursuing a study-abroad experience, the extent to which community colleges actively and aggressively encourage students to seek such an opportunity can affect participation in the program. But encouragement is not enough. Colleges must make education abroad accessible to students. Community colleges that have been most successful in achieving a high level of faculty and student participation in overseas study activities have been able to do the following:

- Establish a program mix to include a variety of education abroad programs—in terms of length, type, location, and discipline— that are appropriate for the institution. A good program mix allows for the greatest number of students to find a program that meets their educational needs and personal circumstances. Course offerings need not be limited to the traditional study-abroad fare of liberal arts and foreign languages. For example, applied science degree programs with very specific and tightly structured curricula, such as nursing and allied health, can develop a meaningful study-abroad course by using a shorter time frame, such as summer or winter. A two-week tour to England focusing on transcultural nursing can look at British nursing practices and education in a multicultural environment through an itinerary of lectures and visits to hospitals, universities, and healthcare centers. Creative solutions could also include experiential learning, distance education modes, and hybrid models (combinations of types of programs).
- Develop and maintain an on-campus international programs office or center to provide essential services to students and faculty. In addition, the person assigned to running this office needs to

be empowered to make the decisions that will get the job done. Administrators should insist that all study-abroad activities go through this office. The days when a professor simply put up a sign to recruit students for his own summer course in Italy should be over. Health, safety, and liability issues dictate that an international programs office, well versed in these issues, be involved in all such efforts.

• Provide a sufficient level of academic and administrative integration with study on campus.

Study-Abroad Program Options

The majority of study-abroad programs that offer college credit are distinguished by three characteristics—length of program, type of program, and how the program is administered at home and abroad.

Length of Program

Academic year programs provide a full year of instruction and credit. A program may correspond to the U.S. calendar in dates and length of time or may, depending on location and type of program, have beginning and end dates far different from the U.S. standard. Many higher education systems outside the United States do not operate in a semester system where students choose courses from a menu of electives. In these cases, both U.S. and host country students follow a prescribed set of subjects or courses and are assessed at the end of the year.

Semester programs generally correspond to the fall and spring semesters and last 12 to 15 weeks. This time frame provides the most flexibility for students by allowing them to take a shorter leave from their study at home and may also be appealing for financial, academic, or personal reasons. Semester models may involve some modification by the host institution to accommodate the study-abroad program, which necessitates a high degree of cooperation between partners.

Summer session programs are four or more weeks in length and may offer a wide variety of learning modes and course offerings. Because the U.S. summer school model is not prevalent in higher education abroad, these are usually separate programs offered exclusively to students from the United States and sometimes other countries.

Short-term study-abroad programs are generally offered during the summer or winter break and are most often study tours led by U.S. college faculty lasting less than four weeks. However, some short-term programs may provide a period of overseas study that is incorporated into a summer session or full semester. That is, a traditional classroom course may have the option of a 10-day field visit over winter or spring break.

Types of Programs

The variety of program types is not limited to those listed below. These types represent the more conventional ones and provide insight into the ways in which overseas academic programs can be organized.

In **host institution–based programs,** the U.S. college negotiates with the institution for students to study in courses provided by the host abroad. U.S. students may study alongside host country nationals, enroll in courses taught by host institution faculty specifically designed for foreign students, take courses taught by home campus faculty at the host institution, or the program may combine elements of all these. Generally, the host institution will also provide on-site orientation student support services, housing assistance, a cultural program, and access to services afforded host country students. In most cases, the U.S. sponsoring institution will issue the official transcript of grades and credits earned based on documentation provided by the host. The U.S. college will pay the host institution a predetermined fee based on the services provided. This model is a one-way flow of students from the United States to abroad but may contain opportunities for faculty exchange or subsidiary student exchanges from the host to the U.S. campus.

In so-called **island programs,** a U.S. college establishes its own overseas study site or center. The U.S. institution rents or owns teaching and living facilities in the host country; hires faculty or provides faculty from the home campus; has complete responsibility for the academic, cultural, and social content and program quality; and provides academic supervision and oversight. These programs are under the full direction of the U.S. campus but may still have some interaction with the host country educational system.

An **exchange program** is generally a bilateral agreement between a U.S. college and an overseas institution for the exchange of students. This model allows for a two-way flow of students between campuses. Students will pay the home campus tuition while attending the partner institution. For community colleges, this can alleviate some of the financial obstacles to study abroad since the cost of tuition will not exceed home campus tuition. However, it also requires that the U.S. institution and the overseas partner have comparable curricula so that the course work taken abroad is relevant to the students' home campus degree. Exchange programs might also require some special payment arrangements, since some state laws might not allow in-state tuition to be used for out-of-country/state students.

Study tours are short-term programs, are usually led by home campus faculty, and can take place in one or more locations abroad. The level of interaction with host country nationals depends on the program design but does not need to be limited to speaking to desk clerks in hotels. On-site activities can include home stays, shadowing exercises (i.e., assignment to a professional in the field of study during the normal work period for a day or so), fieldwork, or extensive site visits, increasing the students' exposure to the host culture.

In **direct enrollment programs,** the student enrolls directly in an overseas institution. It differs from models above in that the home campus may only facilitate the student's enrollment and not have a direct or official relationship with the foreign institution beyond accepting the transfer credit earned. The home campus has no role or only a very limited one in determining the curriculum offered to the student and support services available on-site. The student directly pays a tuition rate established by the overseas institution for "foreign students" and will receive a transcript directly from the host institution.

Internships, practica, service learning, and fieldwork are experiential modes of learning offering academic credit. These experiences can be stand-alone independent studies undertaken by individual students or courses offered or incorporated in any of the program types mentioned above. They can be most effective when the home campus, the student, and the organization overseas work together to structure the experiential work so that it is consistent with the student's educational plan. The next chapter in this book deals more extensively with this type of program.

Program Administration

Study-abroad programs can be administered directly by the U.S. college campus, by a host foreign institution, by an educational organization, by a group of individuals with good contacts in one or more countries, or most often by some combination of these methods. The type of program generally determines how the program is administered. For example, the day-to-day operation of a semester program based at a host institution abroad will be managed by the foreign institution. However, the U.S. sponsor may specify particular features for the program—housing, elective courses, field trips, supplementary language instruction, meal plans, course(s) taught on-site by home campus faculty, faculty or administrative exchanges, and so on—according to the sponsor's requirements. Even in programs primarily administered by the host, the U.S. campus maintains close contact with the overseas institution, directly negotiates fees and services with the host, and is responsible for program oversight. This approach requires regular site visits, program evaluation, and interaction between the partners at several levels—administrative and academic.

Another way a college can run a study-abroad program is to work through a third party to administer and monitor the program abroad. Many such organizations exist and include the Council on International Educational Exchange (CIEE at www.ciee.org), the American Institute for Foreign Study (AIFS at www.aifs.org), and the Centers for Academic Programs Abroad (CAPA at www.capaprograms.org). These organizations and similar ones can provide services for both semester-long and short-term programs and study tours. The U.S. campus, in all of these cases, will be responsible for recruiting and advising students, collecting tuition and fees, processing financial aid, and transcripting the academic work completed.

Not all colleges are prepared to develop or administer programs either on their own or through a third party. However, an institution can still have an extensive program in study abroad by forming partnerships with other institutions. Such a partnership could be a bilateral agreement with another U.S. college to offer its programs to home campus students. Or the campus may join an association of colleges that together offer enrollment opportunities in one another's established study-abroad programs. This consortial approach has the advantage of giving colleges greater control over the quality of the programs offered while also pooling resources. The result is a greater variety of study-abroad opportunities for students and professional development programs for faculty and staff at partner institutions.

The Consortial Approach: One College's Experience

Rockland Community College, State University of New York, is one example of a two-year college that adopted the consortial approach for study abroad early on. In 1968, the college sent its first group of students to England on a faculty-led study tour. In the early 1970s, the college joined with two other community colleges in the region, Mercer Community College in New Jersey and Harrisburg Area Community College in Pennsylvania, to form the Tri-State Consortium. By focusing its efforts on education abroad, the consortium was successful in developing quality low-cost programs and quickly expanded to include more two-year colleges and, eventually, both public and private four-year colleges.

The name of the group was changed in 1975 to the College Consortium for International Studies (CCIS). Today CCIS sponsors 50 education-abroad program sites in 30 countries. Through these programs students could go abroad and, if necessary, study the language at the beginning level while taking other courses taught in English. The CCIS is a consortium that is particularly friendly to community colleges. For a small annual membership fee, a U.S. institution can immediately register and enroll students in semester and summer programs that are sponsored or administered by accredited U.S. colleges.

As a result of using the consortium model, education abroad at Rockland Community College has developed steadily over the last three decades. Currently, the college administers three programs in England for CCIS, operates study tours, conducts professional development activities for its faculty and staff, and works with other community colleges on overseas program development.

On-Campus Considerations

Once a college has determined to make education abroad available and accessible to its students, the decision makers must establish priorities to reflect their level of commitment. The lowest level would be simply to state that the institution encourages students to enroll in approved U.S. college–sponsored study-abroad programs. The college would accept the credit earned in the program for transfer upon submission of the transcript from the administering U.S. institution. The obvious shortcoming is the lack of involvement by the home campus in determining the types of overseas experiences that may be appropriate for their students. It also precludes the type of interaction with colleagues from abroad that results when faculty and staff are directly involved in developing and administering individual or consortial study-abroad programs. Furthermore, students respond enthusiastically to overseas study when the home campus is actively supporting the program and facilitating the student's enrollment. A passive involvement in the study-abroad program on the part of the institution will most likely result in a passive response on the part of students (i.e., low enrollment).

At a minimum, the institution should provide administrative support for the establishment of an international programs office. This is not to be confused with the international student services office, which oversees the needs of foreign students coming to the United States. The exact functions of the international programs office will vary depending on the institution's level of overseas activity. The basic functions would include promoting study abroad, distributing program information, advising students on specific program options, assisting students with applications and financial matters, administering financial aid, facilitating registration of students in study-abroad programs, obtaining course approvals, and, when necessary, evaluating or recommending transfer credit from established programs.

Consideration must also be given to the reporting structure for the international programs office. If the institution is committed to integrating education abroad into the curriculum, then it is essential that the office report to the academic division. The qualifications of the professional staff to run this office should include considerable experience living, traveling, or studying abroad; good communication skills; good organizational ability; academic administration experience; and the ability to effectively interact with faculty and other offices on campus. Study abroad usually involves working out policy and procedures with the academic departments as well as with the registrar, the bursar, the finance office, the financial aid office, the counseling staff, and the transfer adviser. A faculty member or academic administrator with release time may suffice at the beginning, but if the program grows and the institution intends to develop its own overseas study options, then the office will need to devote more time to program administration and management. This will require a commensurate level of resources.

In addition to staffing the office appropriately, the institution must provide a strong level of support for the professional development of staff and other persons involved in education abroad. Two common reasons for failure among nascent efforts to develop overseas program opportunities are (1) lack of support, despite good intentions by the institution, and (2) lack of understanding by the faculty and administration of the multifaceted nature of education abroad. Administering education-abroad efforts is a complex activity requiring broad knowledge not only of the college and its systems but also of overseas educational systems, health and safety concerns, intercultural communication theory, cross-cultural adjustment issues, and more. Much of this knowledge can be learned on the job, through network contacts, and at professional conferences and training sessions.

Links to Study on Campus

Internationalizing the community college campus requires the infusion of international activities throughout the fabric of the institution. We have discussed the importance of linking education abroad with study on campus. Students, faculty, administrators, and trustees—indeed all stakeholders in the institution—need to understand the benefits and importance of international experiences in higher education. For this understanding to occur, study abroad and the course work that results must be solidly linked to the on-campus curriculum:

- Course credit and grades earned in approved study-abroad programs must appear on the student's transcript. The institution must establish relationships with programs abroad, either directly or through consortial relationships that enable the course work to be offered with the same acceptance as on-campus courses. This is not transfer credit but the institution's own credit. Usually this entails the exchange of a memorandum of agreement (MOA) between the U.S. administering campus and the host institution. If the program is part of a consortial arrangement, then the MOA is with the consortium.

- Courses taken abroad must be evaluated to determine ways in which they can satisfy or supplement campus degree requirements. Curriculum committees on campus should be aware that direct equivalencies for overseas courses might not exist, but that course content can be analogous with that of campus-based courses. To enable them to make an informed evaluation, departments should be provided with complete information about overseas courses, including detailed syllabi and the institutions where they are offered.
- Courses must have relevance to home campus curriculum. After the discussion about links to study at the home campus, the importance of this may seem obvious. However, colleges have often initiated discussions with programs in non-English-speaking countries with no consideration for the level of language proficiency or other prerequisites needed for the student to participate.

Contribution to Faculty and Staff Development

The institution should consider ways in which faculty and staff can be involved in program development and oversight or the possibility that exchanges can be arranged between the U.S. campus and the overseas site. The higher the level of involvement of faculty and staff in the organization and administration of education abroad, the more positive and lasting the results will be.

Marketing and Promotion

Colleges usually start an overseas program with the idea of attracting their own students to the program. A variety of promotional techniques are possible. Direct mailings to targeted students, speaking to relevant classes, setting up information tables in high-traffic areas, involving key faculty in the development, and ads and articles in the student newspaper are just a few methods of reaching your potential audience. One of the advantages of belonging to a consortium like CCIS is that ideas about marketing are shared among colleagues. Once programs have been established, many colleges have gone beyond their own campus to recruit students from other colleges. In this case, the overseas program can be used to enhance the revenue stream of the college, a welcome sign to any administrator.

Admission Requirements and Student Selection

Admission criteria and selection methods must be established and agreed upon by both the U.S. institution and the overseas partner. Issues to consider include the following: Are the admission requirements realistic for your student body? If the language of instruction is not English, how will eligibility be determined?

Does your campus determine admission, or will the host reserve the right to final approval? Once determined, the administering campus must clearly articulate the admissions requirements and procedures to students and others involved in the selection process.

Predeparture Preparation Requirements

All study-abroad programs will require predeparture preparation for students. This preparation can take the form of written materials, research or written work, assigned readings, a predeparture orientation meeting, or on-line discussions and activities. Determine the form(s) preparation will take and ensure that the campus has the staff to research, prepare, and update these materials or activities.

Overseas Considerations

Appropriate Staffing at Host Site

There must be trained staff on-site to provide support for students and the faculty who may accompany them. A semester-long program, even one based at a host institution, will require extensive student support services if home stays, cultural visits, "intercambios" (language conversation groups), or other features are organized for U.S. students to meet local college students and interact with the community.

Level of Cultural Interaction with Host Country

Regardless of the length or type of program, cultural interaction with the host country should be incorporated into the program design. Short-term programs need to be creative to ensure that this occurs. For example, a comparative education course abroad may have U.S. students discussing issues in education with a class of their Spanish peers. A performing arts course may engage local actors to conduct a workshop. In longer-term programs, home stays or accommodations in local residences can be arranged. Opportunities for work experience, volunteer activities, and participation in host institution social, sport, and cultural clubs should be available and encouraged.

Noncurricular Considerations: Housing, Meals, and Student Support Services On-Site

It is essential that the U.S. sponsor work out clear policies with the host institution regarding these services. Important factors include the following: What is included in the cost? How is housing selected? What is the standard used in selecting housing? If accommodations are in private houses, how are students assigned? How often are accommodations inspected or visited? What role does the host institution play in resolving conflicts between students and landlords? What meals are provided? What kind of support is available to resolve academic and personal issues and to facilitate integration into the host culture? Does an emergency plan exist in case of political turmoil? In other words, the administering institution must take nothing for granted. However, remember, the purpose of study abroad is not to replicate what is offered on the home campus. A desirable outcome for study abroad is for our students to experience what students in the host country experience to the greatest extent possible.

Other Important Considerations
Health, Safety and Liability Concerns

Addressing issues of student health and safety abroad requires that the international programs office consider a number of areas relevant to their program and its overseas location. The office must (1) gather information on health concerns and medical services of the overseas program location and make this information available to students; (2) collect information from students about their current health status, not for admission purposes but to better advise students and the host overseas; (3) understand the implications of how certain individual health or medical issues—e.g., emotional or mental problems, nutrition, and physical challenges—may be perceived abroad; (4) be prepared to respond quickly and competently to health or safety crises that may occur while their students are abroad; and (5) determine and inform students of medical or travel insurance requirements (Hoffa and Pearson 1997).

These are complex issues that have received significant attention in recent years. Each campus should work out a set of procedures with its host abroad that are to be followed if a perceived or real threat to student safety occurs. These procedures come in handy when international events such as the Gulf War, the bombing in Kosovo, or acts of terrorism occur. The international programs office can monitor what other colleges are doing and get valuable tips on the proper procedures by subscribing to the SECUSS-L e-mail subscription list (see www.secussa.nafsa.org). SECUSSA is the NAFSA group devoted to providing information on education abroad for advisers and program administrators. You can subscribe to the e-mail list without being a member of NAFSA.

Health and safety considerations are invariably connected to issues of institutional liability, and the international programs office must become well informed about ways to minimize the college's exposure to legal action. A reasonably common set of national practices exists for this purpose, and NAFSA and CCIS conferences often have workshops on this topic. The bibliography contains several excellent resources that provide valuable information for an institution planning or reviewing its overseas programs. Also, the University of Southern California (at www.usc.edu/dept/education/gobaled/safeti) provides an excellent Web site for travel and safety information.

Financial Considerations

Developing a short-term or semester program involves considerable costs. Visits to the host site, receiving visits from the host, recruiting and promotion, organizing predeparture preparation, and providing staff and faculty release time are just a few of the planning and start-up costs.

While it is not wise to expect to recover all of the start-up costs in the first year for semester-long programs, this may be necessary for one-time or short-term offerings. In these cases, contracting with an outside agent to arrange the logistics of the study tour is advisable. Building in a small administrative fee to support the on-campus office is common but may have to be limited for one-time, short study tours to keep the price down.

Pricing for ongoing semester programs is another matter. For the first year or two, the program may run at cost or slightly under cost. However, underpricing an overseas program in such a way that it causes a drain on the regular college budget will most certainly raise issues with the college administration. Once they are established, it is not uncommon for summer and semester programs to charge administrative fees in the range of $150 to $500 to help support the cost of overseas program administration. For example, fluctuations in the rate of exchange may affect the final payment sent to the overseas program provider, whether paid in U.S. dollars or foreign currency. In addition, funds must be available for a home campus administrator to visit the program on a regular basis.

While each college will have its own collection and payment methods, most colleges will set up an off-budget account to deal with a significant portion of its overseas finances. Programs that collect money from students to pay for nontuition items, such as housing, meals, and airfare, may not want to run these payments through the regular college budget. Regardless of how the college administers study abroad, it needs to establish appropriate accounting procedures to handle the finances and be prepared to do a proper audit of these funds if they are handled off budget.

Program Review: Outcomes/Assessment Methods

An institution would never develop new degree or campus-based programs without considering ways in which they will be evaluated and how the success of the programs will be determined. This is true for study-abroad programs as well. Campus methods of program evaluation, such as student evaluation, on-site program observations, and cost/benefit analysis can be adapted for overseas programs. Whatever method is chosen, be sure that it is appropriate for the program.

Conclusion

If all of this seems too daunting for a campus to undertake all at once, it may well be. Taking one step at a time, however, the college will grow into the program. As a start, a college can learn a lot by sending someone to a NAFSA meeting in its region (www.nafsa.org). You can certainly talk to colleges in your area about partnering to pool students in joint programs, and you can join a consortium. Whatever you do, it is important that your institution back your efforts and is clear about the level of support it can provide.

Finally, keep in mind that education abroad is but one component in meeting the imperative of internationalizing higher education. The overall effectiveness of education abroad is best accomplished when other aspects of international education as addressed in this volume are applied collegewide. In this way, the academic aspect of the experience abroad is not lost on students when they return home, and the entire campus will benefit from their insight into and enthusiasm for the world beyond their borders.

Bibliography

American Council on International Intercultural Education, Community Colleges for International Development, and The Stanley Foundation. 1998. *Charting the Future of Global Education in the Community College.* New Expeditions Issues Paper No. 2. Washington, D.C.: Community College Press, American Association of Community Colleges.

Blair, Donna, Lisa Phinney, and Kent A. Phillippe. 2001. *International Programs at Community Colleges.* Research Brief AACC-RB-01-1. Washington, D.C.: American Association of Community Colleges.

Burak, Patricia A., and William Hoffa, eds. 2001. *Crisis Management in a Cross-Cultural Setting.* Washington, D.C.: NAFSA: Association of International Educators.

Chase, Audree M., and James R. Mahoney, eds. 1996. *Global Awareness in Community Colleges: A Report of a National Survey.* Washington, D.C.: Community College Press, American Association of Community Colleges.

Davis, Todd M., ed. 1995. *Open Doors 1995/96: Report on International Education Exchange.* New York: Institution of International Education.

_____. 1996. *Open Doors 1996/97: Report on International Education Exchange.* New York: Institution of International Education.

_____. 1997. *Open Doors 1997/98: Report on International Education Exchange.* New York: Institution of International Education.

_____. 1998. *Open Doors 1998/99: Report on International Education Exchange.* New York: Institution of International Education.

_____. 2000. *Open Doors 2000: Report on International Education Exchange.* New York: Institution of International Education.

Hess, J. Daniel. 1997. *Studying Abroad/Learning Abroad.* Yarmouth, Maine: Intercultural Press.

Hoffa, William, and John Pearson, eds. 1997. *NAFSA's Guide to Education Abroad for Advisors and Administrators.* 2d ed. Washington, D.C.: NAFSA: Association of International Educators.

Hoye, William P., and Gary M. Rhodes. 2000. "An Ounce of Prevention Is Worth…the Life of a Student: Reducing Risk in International Programs." *Journal of College and University Law* (summer): 151–185.

Kauffmann, Norman L., Judith N. Martin, and Henry D. Weaver, with Judy Weaver. 1992. *Students Abroad, Strangers at Home: Education for a Global Society.* Yarmouth, Maine: Intercultural Press.

Laubscher, Michael R. 1994. *Encounters with Difference: Student Perceptions of the Role of Out-of-Class Experience in Education Abroad.* Westport, Conn.: Greenwood Press.

Weeks, Kent M. 1999. *Managing Liability and Overseas Programs.* Nashville: College Legal Information.

CHAPTER 5

SERVICE LEARNING ABROAD

Carolyn J. Kadel
Johnson County Community College, Kansas

As community colleges work to educate students about the world and instill a sense of community awareness and responsibility, the merging of overseas study with service learning seems to be a natural development. Including service learning in a study-abroad program offers students an opportunity for focused exposure to the culture, economy, and social structure of the host country. For many students this experience increases global understanding, clarifies career decisions, and solidifies a commitment to social justice (Grusky 2000). Working with such programs offers numerous rewards for students, faculty, and institutions.

What Is Service Learning?

Service learning combines academic disciplines with hands-on experience in relevant service activities. Its advocates in the United States have included William James and John Dewey, and the goal of combining academic work with community service gained numerous supporters in the 1960s and 1970s. The National Community Service Act of 1990 and such programs as Americorps, established in 1993, continued the tradition of supporting and rewarding service among college students (Myers-Lipton 1996, 659). International service learning reflects many of the same influences. In addition, the programmatic work of human-rights, religious, and solidarity organizations during the 1980s propelled the development and influenced the structure and orientation of international service learning programs on many university and college campuses (Grusky 2000). Unlike traditional volunteer service, academic service learning includes assigned readings, discussions, and structured-reflection activities that tie the academic disciplines to the service work. Throughout the literature on service learning, the necessity of reflection is paramount in guiding and focusing the student's learning and problem-solving skills:

> *It is important that programs build structured opportunities for participants to think about their experiences and what they are learning. Through discussion with others and individual reflection on moral questions and relevant issues, participants can develop a better sense of social responsibility,*

advocacy, and active citizenship. This reflective component allows for intel-
lectual growth and development of skills in critical thinking. It is most use-
ful when it is intentional and continuous throughout the experience and
when opportunity for feedback is provided. (Kuprey 1993, 13)

Reflection also works to prevent the reinforcement of prejudice and the development of incorrect assumptions about those in the community being served. In
general, the literature supports the following requirements for successful service
learning, whether domestic or international: the maintenance of academic rigor,
connecting student services with academic courses on service issues, the inclusion
of service learning in course competencies, the necessity of reflection, and evaluation at every level. For "best practices" in community college service learning,
see Robinson and Barnett (1998).

International service learning projects can be included in individual departmental classes or can be administered by two or more departments working
together, and might focus on individual students or promote group activity. They
might be optional or required, but they must reflect the institutional values,
resources, and goals of the home campus. Howard Berry and Linda Chisholm
discuss these issues in useful detail in *Service Learning in Higher Education around
the World: An Initial Look* (1999).

Why Service Learning?

Those who support service learning in higher education "believe that it stimulates
academic performance, increases students' understanding of the responsibilities
of living in a democratic society, and encourages students to become involved in
the social problems facing their communities" (Gray et al. 1999, 2). In the 1999
evaluation of the $10 million Learn and Serve America, Higher Education
(LSAHE) program, the results pointed to increased civic responsibility on the
part of students. Student academic work improved if the service occurred for
more than 20 hours per week, was integrated into the course content, and included structured reflection on the experience (Gray et al. 1999).

Other research supports the contention that "students who are involved in
service learning show larger increases in international understanding than students involved in voluntarism or no service" (Myers-Lipton 1996, 3). In addition
to having positive effects on student performance and development, service learning can improve community relations, stimulate faculty development, and
encourage innovation in the curriculum. "In the end," write Berry and Chisholm,
"the impact of service learning is deeper even than connections made between
studies and service, college and community, theory and practice, earning and

doing. Service learning has to do with attitudes and behaviors that lie at the root of how a society functions" (1999, 93).

Successful international service programs require many of the same components as traditional study-abroad programs and domestic service projects: serious orientation for students, well-established connections with host sites and agencies, rigorous monitoring of student experiences and academic progress, and thoughtful reentry programs. The service experience also puts students in contact with particular segments of host societies that traditional study-abroad programs might not. According to service learning researcher Sara Grusky, "[W]hether the service learning experience propels one to enter a new neighborhood or travel thousands of miles to a new country, issues of cultural arrogance, racism, stereotypes, privilege, and economic disparity will have to be discussed" (2000, 3). In programs that prepare and guide students through these issues, the results are life changing.

Academic/Service Opportunities for Community College Students

For community colleges interested in offering international service opportunities to their students, several good choices exist that require minimal institutional or administrative resources. Both the International Partnership for Service Learning and the College Consortium for International Studies offer complete "packages" of academic service learning opportunities.

International Partnership for Service Learning (IPSL)

Founded in 1982, IPSL offers semester-long and summer programs for students in 11 countries—the Czech Republic, Ecuador, France, India, Israel, Jamaica, Mexico, the Philippines, Russia, United Kingdom, and Vietnam—and in South Dakota with Native Americans. IPSL is perhaps the best-known organization working in this area and offers quality programs that combine academic rigor with significant service assignments. Students in the Partnership programs perform service 15 to 20 hours per week in projects that are directly connected to academic courses. Students earn 12 to 16 credits a semester, or 6 to 12 for a summer program. Participants are placed in local agencies with skilled professionals who understand the problems and culture of the local community. Their academic work is supervised by faculty from the host culture, and most universities and U.S. colleges accept the credit earned during the Partnership experience. Students are housed with local families or with local students. According to IPSL literature, 80 percent of Partnership students are undergraduates, and community college students are welcome to participate.

Community college study-abroad or service learning directors can work directly with IPSL to find programs to meet the needs of their students and may send one or more qualifying students on IPSL programs. IPSL arranges course offerings, student service placements, and housing for participating students. On-site program directors assist students with orientation and adjustment issues. IPSL provides attractive and informative recruitment materials for use by individual campuses. Once interested students are identified, most details are arranged by the Partnership. Since the awarding of credit and the possibility of financial aid are almost always important to students, it is imperative that the local college officials understand and develop policy on these issues. As with other study-abroad programs, students in approved programs are eligible for financial aid if they remain registered at their home institution. Students who are co-enrolled at their home colleges and in IPSL programs receive credit upon completion of the program. Although individual colleges accomplish this in a variety of ways, it is not a difficult task to work through. Positive results do require that the study-abroad director or service learning coordinator work with the campus financial aid office and with the registrar to ensure that aid and credits are appropriately provided. If institutional obstacles prohibit such policies, students may opt for the official transfer of credits or for an international service experience that does not result in academic credit.

IPSL organizes conferences that explore both the practical and the theoretical aspects of international service. It also publishes books for both students and faculty, provides a short video on IPSL programs, and publishes a semiannual newsletter, *Action/Reflection,* that features articles on international service learning issues. Information on IPSL programs and publications can be found on its Web site listed under Resources at the end of this chapter.

College Consortium for International Studies (CCIS)

CCIS includes service learning options in several of its overseas programs. As with IPSL, CCIS provides community colleges with programs in which most of the logistics are carried out by the CCIS-sponsoring institution. For campuses with limited resources or a small number of students ready to study abroad, these programs provide opportunities without pressing the resources of the local campus. Financial aid and credit issues need to be resolved by the home institution, but issues of orientation, housing, course and service selection, and oversight are accomplished through CCIS. Two of the CCIS service learning programs in developing countries are discussed briefly below. Other programs can be found on the Web site listed under Resources.

In Ecuador, CCIS sponsors for this program are Brookdale Community College, New Jersey, and the College of Staten Island/CUNY, New York. Students who select the program in Guayaquil, Ecuador, may enroll in a sociology course called Contemporary Ecuadorian Society that includes a service learning component. This course examines sociocultural, historical, political, and economic issues in Ecuador and places students in schools or service agencies for a minimum of five hours per week. Although this course provides less time spent in service than IPSL programs do, it does provide students with hands-on service experience that is processed within the parameters of academic course work. In addition to the service course, students also study Spanish and other courses with Latin American content at the Universidad Catolica de Santiago de Guayaquil.

In the Dominican Republic, Broome Community College, New York, sponsors the CCIS program through Pontificia Universidad Catolica Madre y Maestra in Santo Domingo, where individual students may enroll in either the fall or the spring semester. As part of the course work for the semester, students must enroll in a three-credit course on Dominican society and culture, and they have the option of enrolling in a three-credit community service course. Through this service learning course students complete approximately 100 hours of guided community service in various agencies serving children, women, and environmental issues. As with the IPSL and CCIS programs in Ecuador, the service sites are community-based organizations run by local residents or agencies.

Service Organizations

The programs discussed above combine academic and service learning components in one package. Some community colleges may wish to develop the academic component of a program but may hesitate to take on the many details of organizing the international service activities. In this case, numerous organizations exist that routinely sponsor service experiences with whom a community college may work to create a short-term international experience.

Global Volunteers, a private nonprofit organization founded in 1984, is an example of such a resource. Global Volunteers has sites in 19 countries and in 19 states in the United States. This organization provides orientation materials about its specific projects, information and advice about supplies, cultural information about the host site, and is responsible for food and lodging logistics. Participants pay an administrative fee for these services. Programs focusing on childcare, English language acquisition, and construction are organized for from one to three weeks. Campus responsibilities would include recruitment of staff and students, academic connections, predeparture meetings, reflection in the field, and posttrip activities. Information about Global Volunteers can be found on their Web site listed under Resources.

Peacework is another nonprofit organization that arranges international projects for college and community groups. The organization has sites in 20 countries and arranges housing, food, travel, and support materials. Projects usually last from one to three weeks and include both hands-on service and cultural programs. The work sites are coordinated by local organizations and include work with institutions serving children and construction or renovation work. Fees include the actual cost of all arrangements and supplies plus an administrative fee. Most recently the organization has worked with housing and school construction projects in Honduras, Guatemala, Haiti, Belize, Russia, Vietnam, and China. Information about Peacework can be found on their Web site listed under Resources.

Amizade Volunteer Programs is a nonprofit organization begun in 1994 with international programs in Brazil, Bolivia, Australia, and the Navajo Nation. The organization can customize activities (construction, health centers, reforestation projects), accommodations (hotels, cabins, tents), and length of stay (seven days to three months). The organization has access to local professionals in many fields including healthcare, education, welfare, and the environment. Panel discussions and site observations can be arranged. Language programs are incorporated in programs in Brazil, Bolivia, and the Navajo Nation. Program costs vary depending on the above factors, and each group is asked to contribute to the cost of the program materials and supplies for the projects. For more information see Resources.

Campuses without host site connections who want to take groups abroad may find agencies such as Global Volunteers, Peacework, or Amizade a practical way to begin. Check the International Volunteer Programs Association Web site (www.volunteerinternational.org) for a list of other organizations that organize international projects for individuals or groups. In addition, individual students can perform well-monitored quality service through such organizations as Operation Crossroads in Africa (see Resources). If resources and interest are limited, a department might consider independent study credit for those who combine such service with structured readings and reflection assignments.

Creating Your Own Program

For campuses interested in creating an international service program, the rewards, and the challenges, can be great. The hours spent finding and monitoring a reliable service site, facilitating the academic connections, securing funding, and networking across campus can be daunting. But the impact such a program will have on faculty, staff, and student development, the cross-institutional connections it will create, and the opportunities for meaningful service it will provide can make the time spent worthwhile. Since community college students often have limited resources or have family obligations, jobs, or other impediments to semester-long study abroad, short intensive projects that combine predeparture orientation and on-site reflection offer meaningful opportunities. Below are some examples of campus-grown programs.

Johnson County Community College, Kansas

Like many other institutions, Johnson County Community College (JCCC) in Overland Park, Kansas, has a well-established international program and a more recent, but quite successful, service learning program. These two programs coexisted more or less separately until 1996. Brought together by JCCC's Center for Teaching and Learning and using travel funds provided by a grant to the AACC from the Corporation for National Service, a joint project developed a service site in Guadalajara, Mexico. The site, Centro Integral Comunitario, had experience with individual IPSL students but had never worked with a larger group of students and had no experience arranging short, intensive projects, with housing, food, supplies, and transit for an incoming group. JCCC had previous experience sending students abroad and had some experience with domestic service learning within academic classes but had no previous experience organizing an international service project that was cocurricular. Novices reigned on both sides, but enthusiasm overcame many obstacles.

The initial pilot project, the construction of a security wall, was designed to be short and outside the regular curriculum, although orientation and reflection were important components. Faxes, letters, and visits to Guadalajara took place during an 18-month period to develop the work project and to grapple with room-and-board issues, supplies, and other on-site issues. On the JCCC campus, recruitment concentrated on students from the college honors program, the student senate, the international club, and on students who were involved in service learning classes. Funding for faculty and students required cooperation among the divisions of International Education, Service Learning, Student Life, and the honors program. Orientation meetings familiarized students with aspects of Mexican culture, the culture of poverty, the art of bricklaying, and team-building exercises. Students solicited donations and supplies from area businesses, civic organizations, and churches; and faculty and staff worked to gain publicity through press releases and college publications. In May 1998, a group of 12 students and 6 staff members set off to construct a security wall that would allow a community center and clinic to provide regular service to the impoverished community of Santa Rosa. In addition, the group took medical supplies, shoes, and clothing for community residents. The project lasted two weeks and included a diverse group of students, the director of International Education, JCCC's staff photographer, a counselor, and professors of heating, ventilation, and air conditioning; nursing; and sociology. While the particular composition of the staff group was largely unplanned, it was an important reason for the continuing success of the project.

The following year, the now veteran nursing professor organized a group focused on healthcare that worked closely with community residents, completing

180 home visits, assisting with 150 clinic visits, and teaching local residents preventative health measures. Photos and public presentations from the first trip were important in publicizing the program and building campus enthusiasm for the project. In 2000, the college sent two groups, one composed mainly of nursing students, the second focusing mainly on dental hygiene and bringing in faculty and students who were new to the experience. In 2001, another two groups made the journey, bringing in faculty in child development and foreign languages.

The rewards of creating a program from scratch are numerous. Student responses to this program have been overwhelmingly enthusiastic, and many of the 95 students who have participated in it have described the program as the highlight of their college experience. Students, including even some nonparticipants, worked together on campus to raise funds and supplies. The project stimulated a new and contagious cooperation among the staff. The college received positive publicity in the community and was able to involve community representatives in fundraising for the project. Disciplines and departments that had not been involved in either international programs or service projects became active. Based on the overwhelmingly positive response, the college institutionalized the program through its budget process. Participating staff members receive grants to cover their expenses for transportation, housing, and food. Students receive partial funding through student activities funds. Fundraising projects begin early in the year and pay almost all remaining fees.

The challenges of creating such a program are significant. Finding an appropriate and responsible host site is critical to the success of the program and the well-being of the participants. Secure housing, well-conceived projects, and attention to the numerous details of any work project are important. Preplanning and gathering support within the institution cannot be underestimated. Orientation to the project and to the culture must be thorough, and all aspects of the program must reinforce flexibility and tolerance for ambiguity.

Colleges should start small, allow sufficient lead time, gather as much information as possible about participants, choose and orient students carefully, learn as much as possible about the service site and project, and strive for support from the whole college. Be certain all participants have adequate medical coverage and that the site is prepared for emergencies and illness. The academic focus must be strong and well planned. Involve other faculty and staff in the planning and implementation so that the existence of the project does not depend on one or two individuals, and work to institutionalize the program as soon as possible.

JCCC's program began as a cocurricular project. As such, it originally concentrated most on the service aspect. Although this was a good beginning, the connection with concepts from academic disciplines needed to be strengthened.

After the first year, the project was offered for independent study credit or as fulfillment of an honors contract in the nursing program. In the future, students will enroll in a required predeparture course on Mexican culture and poverty in developing societies to ensure that each group of participating students has an appropriate foundation on which to base its reflections.

Colorado Mountain College

The Service Learning Abroad program at Colorado Mountain College (CMC) is based in Nicaragua and El Salvador. Reflecting on the history and development of the project, Dave Harmon, the faculty leader, reports that the project developed from a fall 1989 ethics course in which the class discussed the possibility of travel and service in a Third World country. The idea was implemented in the summer of 1990 when six CMC students and their professor traveled to northern Nicaragua. In addition to the travel, faculty and students also created a student club, the World Awareness and Action Society; a World Hunger Conference; a World Hunger Seminar; and a speaker's series on related issues. Since 1998, the trip has been a three-credit course at the college (Anthropology 221–Cultural Studies 1–Service Learning Abroad) and now includes El Salvador as a destination. In addition to the travel segment of the course, which includes home stays with Salvadoran families, the course requires participation in daily reflection sessions, the completion of book reviews before departure, service in the Salvadoran community, daily journal entries, and a final paper upon return.

Harmon reports that as the program developed, several sources helped promote its success. First, the Student Club helped create interest in the World Hunger Seminar. The seminar, in turn, created opportunities for students to learn about and experience service learning. Returning students, inspired and energized by their experiences, became more involved with the program on CMC's campus. Currently, because of increased costs and decreased institutional budgets, staff at CMC are working to create an enterprise to fund service learning from new private partnerships. For more information, see Resources.

Southwestern College, California

The Baja California Studies program at Southwestern College (SWC) offers an interdisciplinary approach to intercultural education that includes a service learning requirement. The program is designed to offer a study-abroad experience for students who lack the time or money for more extensive travel and to educate SWC students about their neighboring communities to the south. Students may earn a basic (12 credits) or an advanced (18 credits) certificate that includes courses focusing on Baja California. The courses are taught on SWC's campus, in service learning projects in the border communities of Baja California, and through a summer Spanish language program taught in Baja. On-campus courses include offerings from biology, art, communications, and literature. This program was developed by an ad hoc committee of SWC instructors and administrators intent on incorporating the rich culture of Baja into the SWC curriculum. Initially perceived as a summer program, the concept was expanded to a certificate program that combines language and culture studies with service. SWC's partner college in Mexico, the Universidad Autonoma de Baja California in La Paz, assists with the program activities in Mexico. For more information about the SWC program, see Resources.

Kapi`olani Community College, Hawaii

Linda Fujikawa had sponsored language and culture tours to Japan before she developed a service learning project in 1997. Familiarity with the culture and specific contacts in Japan made the inclusion of a service component easier. Students prepared for the project by spending the academic year teaching Japanese at Waialea Elementary School in Hawaii. The students used storytelling, songs, and other activities in their instruction. On the basis of their skill and commitment, the six students involved were invited to participate in the summer project at Cozen Elementary School in Automata, Kanazawa, a remote papermaking village in Japan, where children had had little opportunity to interact with native speakers of English. Because of the small size of the group, the town was able to accommodate it in a 500-year-old Buddhist temple. The students taught English daily and performed English and Hawaiian songs and dances for the entire village on Saturday. During the second week, the group traveled to Kanazawa Institute of Technology in the city. Here, the service group met with high school students daily and helped them practice their conversational skills. Kapi`olani's project now offers students the opportunity to go individually to assist with English instruction at the Midorigaoka Preschool in Kanazawa in exchange for a home stay. Students perform two weeks of service with free room and board.

Conclusion

Service learning and international education are each an important and vital part of education in the 21st century. Combined, these programs create an exceptional opportunity for students to learn by doing, to understand the significance of culture by meeting and knowing others, and to apply their academic knowledge to problems that continue to destabilize the world. Because the intercultural literacy resulting from such programs is important to the future of our students, community colleges can make an enormous contribution by developing and guiding such programs.

Programs need not be expensive or complicated in their approach. But they must be meaningful in their work, in their reflective components, and in the extent to which they involve local communities in their planning and implementation.

Bibliography

Berry, Howard A., and Linda Chisholm. 1999. *Service Learning in Higher Education around the World: An Initial Look.* New York: International Partnership for Service Learning.

Gray, Maryann, et al. 1999. *Combining Service and Learning in Higher Education.* Summary report. Washington, D.C: Rand.

Grusky, Sara. 2000. "International Service Learning: A Critical Guide from an Impassioned Advocate." *American Behavioral Scientist* 43 (February): 858–867.

Kuprey, Tamar Y., ed. 1993. *Rethinking Tradition: Integrating Service with Academic Study on College Campuses.* Providence: Education Commission of the States.

Myers-Lipton, Scott J. 1996. "Effect of Service Learning on College Students' Attitudes toward International Understanding." *Journal of College Student Development* 37 (November/December).

Robinson, Gail, and Lynn Barnett. 1998. *Best Practices in Service Learning: Building a National Community College Network, 1994–1997.* Project Brief AACC-PB-98-3. Washington, D.C.: American Association of Community Colleges.

Resources

The book listed below deserves special attention as a resource guide. It provides critical reviews of more than 100 volunteer-abroad programs. The other resources below are Web sites of the organizations referred to in this chapter.

- Collins, Joseph, S. DeZerega, and Z. Heckscher. 2002. *How to Live Your Dream of Volunteering Overseas.* New York: Penguin Books.
- Amizade Volunteer Programs: www.amizade.org
- College Consortium for International Studies: www.ccisabroad.org
- Colorado Mountain College: www.coloradomtn.edu/international.html
- Global Volunteers: www.globalvolunteers.org
- International Partnership for Service Learning: www.ipsl.org
- Operation Crossroads in Africa: www.igc.org/oca
- Peacework: www.peacework.org
- Southwestern College: www.swc.cc.ca.us/~mstinson
- www.volunteeroverseas.org

CHAPTER 6

PARTNERSHIPS ABROAD:
TECHNICAL ASSISTANCE AND BEYOND

John Halder
Community Colleges for International Development, Iowa

There is no question that community colleges have opportunities to develop partnerships with institutions abroad on their own. Frequently, however, individual colleges find that they do not have the experience, funding, or personnel to undertake the kind of development projects that foreign partners need, particularly in the area of technical and vocational education. For this reason, individual colleges may find it advantageous to cooperate in undertaking such projects. By combining their expertise with others', a broader range of opportunities for faculty development can be provided and valuable international experiences can benefit all involved. Such was the vision of Max King, then president of Brevard Community College in Florida, when he started Community Colleges for International Development (CCID) in 1977.

Today, CCID is a nonprofit corporation comprising approximately 100 colleges. CCID's purpose is to assist community colleges in internationalizing their campuses by providing faculty with opportunities to engage in international training activities. By facilitating these training activities, CCID has assisted its member colleges in developing partnerships abroad that yield benefits both within and outside the CCID family. Just as the community colleges in their home communities are seen as training authorities for business and industry, international clients increasingly view the community college model as offering them distinct advantages over the technical and vocational training systems they have in place. When seeking funding from an agency to engage in an overseas project, CCID can marshal the combined resources of its members, which represent more than 300 vocational and technical programs and more than 9,000 faculty and staff. Whether the client is an individual college, a government ministry, a business entity, an international nongovernmental organization (NGO), or one of the development banks, CCID has a remarkable set of resources to bring to the table.

This chapter will illustrate, through case studies, some of the many partnerships and training activities undertaken by CCID and its member colleges during the past few years.

CCID Organizational Structure

CCID's organizational structure facilitates the development of partnerships for its member colleges. The small central office, located at Kirkwood Community College in Iowa, serves as a clearinghouse for CCID activities and plans events. As president of the organization I frequently visit funding agencies and report back to the members on the possibilities for new initiatives. The members have organized themselves into both regional subcommittees and subject subcommittees. Regional subcommittees cover Latin America, the Caribbean, India, Asia, Russia, Africa, Europe/Eastern Europe, and the Near/Middle East.

To facilitate networking and the formation of partnerships, CCID holds an annual conference in the winter that is open to both members and nonmembers. It also sponsors a summer institute that is limited to members and invited guests and allows time for planning and internal governance activities. Both meetings are held in places where foreign partners and members can meet with representatives from a variety of potential funding agencies.

On occasion, the CCID central office will seek out a funding opportunity itself and offer it to the members who are willing and able to serve as a lead institution for that project. Since the presidents of the member colleges are actively involved in the organization through the CCID board of directors, they often set a direction and initiate activity, leaving it to the membership and its committees to follow up. On other occasions, members bring projects to the board with which they need help. If the board approves, it might supply seed money, usually in the form of travel grants, to support the development of the partnership. If the partnership develops, the board may invite the foreign partners to one of the CCID conferences to meet the members and to allow for the necessary networking.

As an example, CCID had a faculty exchange agreement with several universities in Eastern Europe that went back to 1987. With the fall of communism, the presidents decided that an expansion in the area was necessary. In 1991, a group of presidents visited Bulgaria, Romania, and Yugoslavia and signed a series of agreements to explore new avenues of cooperation. Rectors from the University of Bucharest and the University of Craiova in Romania were invited to the 1992 winter conference in California. Broome Community College in New York soon formed a partnership with these two universities. With assistance from its foreign partners, Broome secured funding from the USIA and the Soros Foundation to engage in a project that ran from 1993 to 1996. Broome became the lead college, but four other CCID colleges also participated in the project to help the Romanian universities upgrade their business and economics programs.

On another occasion, after the North American Trade Agreement (NAFTA) was signed, CCID sought ways to facilitate partnerships between its Canadian and

U.S. members with institutions in Mexico. One such partnership, established by Austin Community College, Texas, is described in chapter 7. The CCID board moved the winter 2000 meeting to Monterey, Mexico, to allow potential Mexican partners easier access to CCID members and services. Likewise, the 2001 summer institute was held at the East-West Center at the University of Hawaii so that CCID members could meet with a group of 25 Japanese junior college presidents who were interested in developing partnerships.

The case studies that follow provide other examples of how CCID works as a facilitator of overseas partnerships for its members.

India

CCID has had a 20-year history of working in India. In recent years, leadership has been provided equally by Eastern Iowa Community College District (EICCD), Iowa, and Sinclair Community College (SCC), Ohio, but faculty from other CCID colleges have also been involved. Early CCID India activities included Fulbright exchanges and the hosting of Indian education delegations sponsored by the World Bank, the University Grants Commission, and the archbishop of Madras. CCID also sponsored a U.S. community college delegation to India, conducted workshops in India on community colleges, and created working partnerships between higher education and the business community. Recent completed and current CCID projects include the following:

- In fall 2000, CCID completed a series of four one-day workshops. Designed for business, government, and educators, they were held in the cities of Chennai, Trivandrum, Hyderabad, and Bangalore. They focused on the development of relevant workforce training in India and the potential for partnerships with U.S. colleges.
- In January 2000, CCID established an office in India under the direction of Adrian Almeida, who served as project director for the Center for Vocational Education (CVE) in Madras and as the first president of the Madras Community College. This office is linking CCID with educational institutions and businesses in India. EICCD acts as the liaison with the India office.
- In 1997, the USAID University Linkage Project was completed. This five-year project, valued at $750,000 with an equal match, was directed by Sinclair Community College and codirected by EICCD. It brought 15 vocational/technical faculty members from eight CCID colleges to the CVE in Madras. These faculty members, working with Indian partners, developed vocational training

programs aimed at school dropouts, rural and urban poor, and women with limited opportunities.

- The USIA University Affiliations Project, valued at $120,000 for three years, was directed by Sinclair Community College. It involved the exchange of faculty from Stella Maris College, Madras, with faculty from Sinclair and EICCD. The project strengthened literacy education in the United States and India.
- The two-year U.S. Department of Education–Title VI-B Business Linkage Project, directed by EICCD, strengthened international business education at U.S. community colleges and promoted trade relationships between companies in India and the United States. EICCD led a trade mission of small and medium-size businesses to India in fall 1996. This project is described in chapter 9.
- As a direct result of the success of CVE in Madras, the religious, political, and business leaders of Madras stepped forward to support the creation of Madras Community College—an innovative, community-driven, higher education institution.
- The Ford Motor Company entered into a joint venture with Mahindra Motors to establish a major automobile manufacturing plant near Madras. The key players for establishing a training center for automotive excellence were identified, and this collaborative effort was implemented in January 1997.
- A conference held in Madras, "Training for Early School Leavers," was developed jointly by CVE, Sinclair Community College, and EICCD. The conference focused world attention on the plight of the early school leaver. Teaching/learning experiments that promote training and education for this population were shared.

CCID continues to work with colleagues in India and to search for opportunities to continue the partnerships that have been established.

Caribbean Region
Because of the Caribbean's proximity to the United States, many colleges have an interest in the region. Below are descriptions of a few of the CCID activities that have taken place here for many years.

Aruba
A recent CCID project involved training for the Ministry of Education in Aruba. In this instance, the lead colleges were Eastern Iowa Community College

District, Iowa, and Kirkwood Community College, Iowa. The funding for this activity was obtained from the Ministry of Education, Aruba.

CCID was invited to visit Aruba to evaluate the needs of the country as it combined four technical/vocational colleges into a national community college. Through a series of meetings with the minister for education and the consultant charged with implementing the system, an action plan was developed to address the identified needs. This plan included arranging for the principal of the newly created national community college to get in-service training at selected CCID colleges. The new principal's attendance at the CCID annual conference to network and develop relationships was an important part of this process and allowed the necessary partnerships to develop. As a result, the training outcomes were achieved in all of the fields promised the grantor.

Caribbean Conference

In 1998, CCID organized a conference in Suriname. At this conference, 14 CCID colleges worked with 13 Caribbean countries to identify the development needs of the 14 countries in the Caribbean community (CARICOM), to propose options to meet those identified needs, and to develop an action plan to respond to the identified needs. The conference was funded by the Organization of American States (OAS); the Ministry of Education, Suriname; the Ministry of Education, Guyana; the company Telesur, Suriname; and CCID.

Following the conference, six major issues were identified and a draft plan for each was developed:

- Technical Teacher Training
- Training Standards and Certification
- Technical Vocational Education and Training (TVET) and Business/Industry Partnerships
- Development of Shared National Databases
- TVET Governance
- Improving the Image of TVET

This is a major project for which increased funding is currently being sought. In the long term, CCID hopes to assist the countries of CARICOM by providing a strategy and a connection with global funding sources that will assist these nations in developing a trained workforce, establishing international standards, and increasing the quality and productivity of their products and services.

Guyana

A highly successful project, initiated by St. Louis Community College, used the resources of various other CCID colleges in Guyana. Known as Guyana Technical College Skill Upgrading, it was funded through the University Development Linkage Project of the U.S. Agency for International Development (USAID).

The project came about through the efforts of international education specialists at St. Louis Community College responding to a Sister Cities initiative. In the early stages, a representative of the college traveled to Guyana and began working with representatives of the Guyanese Ministry of Education. It was determined that certain programs at the seven Guyanese technical colleges were in need of upgrading and that there was a match between them and many of the colleges represented in CCID.

A project was designed so that Guyanese faculty would be selected to travel to CCID colleges for internships, followed by their U.S. mentors returning to Guyana to provide in-service training. Working in conjunction with the minister of education, the project leaders chose 11 technical areas for renewal, ranging from agricultural mechanics to the maintenance and repair of electronic equipment.

In the United States, an advisory team was created for the project, consisting of the presidents of the U.S. colleges participating in the program. With their assistance, funding totaling $1,403,000 over a five-year period was obtained. In total, nine CCID colleges were heavily involved in this project.

As a result of this project the following outcomes were achieved:

- Sixteen Guyanese faculty and staff members completed attachments at CCID colleges. Each attachment was defined by realistic goals, which were attained. The topics included best teaching practices, academic administration, mig and tig welding, electrical installation, introduction to Microsoft Office, and others.
- Fifteen workshops delivered by CCID faculty members have been completed. More than 200 staff members from the Guyana technical institutes have attended. Most of the participants have obtained in-service credit toward certification in these workshops.
- More than 20 CCID staff members have worked in Guyana during the five years of this project, adding to the globalization of CCID staff members and their respective colleges.

- Additional activities spun off this project include the shipment of more than 180,000 pounds of donated surplus equipment. This equipment was secured by participating CCID colleges and has included books, auto engines, furniture, more than 80 computers, metal-shop equipment, and electronic equipment.

Latin America

Many CCID member colleges have Latin American student populations and enjoy developing relationships with their countries of origin. One project resulting from such a relationship is the activity with Universidad Don Bosco, El Salvador.

Universidad Don Bosco

This project represented an innovative technical assistance program that began in February 1996 and ended December 1998. It involved 30 consultants from 10 CCID colleges, and the Universidad Don Bosco (UDB) in El Salvador. The German development bank, Kreditanstalt für Wiederaufbau (KfW), provided $225,000 to CCID for this project with a match equivalent to approximately double that amount coming from the member colleges that worked on the project.

The purpose of the program was to provide UDB with consulting and advising expertise in the formulation of diagnostics, projects, strategic plans of action, and implementation of recommendations made by CCID senior educational and technical experts. The program provided a professional development opportunity for faculty consultants, primarily Hispanic, from community colleges and universities in the United States, Canada, and Puerto Rico. UDB staff participated in orientation and training visits at counterpart institutions in the United States and Canada. These visits provided UDB with well-grounded models to assist in its development.

The program was ambitious in scope. The initial goal was to complete the entire program in 24 months, with approximately 20 CCID experts involved in five major areas. In fact, the program lasted 34 months and involved 30 experts on-site at UDB, with dozens more providing support at their respective home institutions.

The initial lead institution for the UDB program was Daytona Beach Community College, Florida. In 1998, the lead was transferred to Rancho Santiago Community College District (RSCCD) in Santa Ana, California.

The UDB/CCID program operated as a performance-based agreement under a Task Order concept with specific sets of priorities to be accomplished by the expert(s). For each assignment, UDB issued a Task Order designating the scope of work required by the experts. The CCID lead institution was required to respond to each Task Order within 30 days by showing the action to be taken, the personnel to be provided, the duration of task performance, and other information.

A written report outlining the scope of work accomplished was provided within 20 days of the return of the consultant. The reports often provided materials for follow-up visits or contingency orders that had not been identified in the initial proposal.

Follow-up visits by either a consultant or the program manager ensured continuity of recommendations and suggestions made during the Task Order visits. This process enabled UDB to implement recommendations in a timely manner, building on each successive Task Order.

The case studies just presented are examples of projects that have either been completed or are in mature stages of operation. The case study below, of a Russian/Norwegian partnership, is an example of a new initiative in its early stages of development. As can be seen by the sequence of dates, projects like these sometimes take a long time to develop.

Russia/Norway

On January 11, 1993, a multilateral cooperative agreement within the region of the Barents Sea was formalized by the establishment of the Barents Euro-Arctic Region (BEAR). This agreement, the Kirkenes Declaration, was signed by the foreign ministers of Finland, Norway, Sweden, and Russia, as well as by representatives of Denmark, Iceland, and the European Union. The signing was attended by observers from the United States, Canada, France, Japan, Poland, Great Britain, and Germany.

During the mid-1990s, CCID and Niels Brock College, Copenhagen, Denmark (International Member, CCID), worked on the feasibility of establishing an educational and economic development linkage to the Barents Group, a part of KPMG Consulting. If such a linkage was possible, then CCID members would be able to become involved in a number of activities with members of the group.

In June 1998, a representative of CCID attended a conference in Kirkenes, Norway, to help develop the framework and plans for establishing a partnership. The conference was hosted by Ms. Oddrunn Pettersen, Norway's general secretary for BEAR. The conference was attended by high government officials and key educational leaders from Norway, Denmark, the Faeroe Islands, Finland, Sweden, Russia, Iceland, Greenland, and other countries. From this point a series of events has led to a stronger connection between CCID and the Barents Secretariat. Among these are the following:

- **Activities in 1998.** At the CCID summer conference, the board of directors approved funding of $4,500 to develop an educational mission to Denmark and Norway. The purpose of the mission was to explore and establish a memorandum of understanding and agreements between the Barents Group and CCID. Targeted programs for the Barents region were in the areas of distance education, small business development, health, fisheries, and technology, among others.
- **Activities in 1999.** At the January CCID annual conference the Barents Secretariat signed a memorandum of understanding with CCID, each party agreeing to develop further projects and activities. In late September/early October 1999, three CCID members traveled to Kirkenes, Norway, and then to Murmansk, Russia, to discuss with the Norwegian and Russian partners possible strategies for the next level of activities.
- **Most recent activities (autumn 2000–present).** It was agreed that the U.S. colleges expressing interest in this project would travel to Europe to meet their Russian counterparts. The Barents Secretariat made the arrangements, and in October 2000 representatives from seven CCID community colleges traveled first to St. Petersburg and then by train to Petrozavodsk, Russia, for a three-day conference. The CCID board of directors supported this initiative for their member colleges through a series of small minigrants to support travel expenses. Through this process, the following alignment of colleges and projects has developed:
  – Broome (New York) will work on a distance-learning project with four Russian and three Norwegian colleges. Green River (Washington), Daytona Beach (Florida), and Kapi`olani (Hawaii) will work on programs in entrepreneurship and tourism with two Russian and two Norwegian colleges. Northampton (Pennsylvania) and Kapi`olani (Hawaii) will work on an English-as-a-second-language (ESL) program with three Russian colleges and the Kirkenes Adult Education Center, Norway. Northampton (Pennsylvania) will work on an early-childhood-education program with one Russian and two Norwegian colleges. Southwest Virginia will work on a cultural exchange with one Russian and one Norwegian college, and Monroe (Rochester, New York) will work on an alcohol and drug prevention program with one Russian and one Norwegian college. A grant team from the CCID member colleges is currently working to review possible funding sources for these activities.

Conclusion

The case studies in this chapter represent a sample of the activities undertaken by CCID in the past few years. It is not a comprehensive list of all of the partnerships that member colleges have developed, nor does it represent the entire range of activities that CCID has historically undertaken. For instance, in the early history of the organization, faculty exchanges were more common than they are today. From 1986 to 1989, 18 faculty members from colleges in Taiwan spent a semester or more as visiting professors at CCID colleges. This program was entirely financed by the Taiwanese government. From 1987 to 1998, more than 300 professional exchanges for a semester or more were arranged by CCID between member colleges and university partners in Russia and Eastern Europe. The demand for these kinds of exchanges has diminished over the past few years, and the exchange program is now in abeyance. In response, CCID has shifted its efforts into the type of development activities described in this chapter.

In the future, CCID will strive to maintain a flexible organization that will respond to the demands of its members in facilitating global partnerships. The CCID Web site, www.ccid.kirkwood.cc.ia.us, provides additional information.

CHAPTER 7

PARTNERSHIPS ABROAD: CURRICULUM DEVELOPMENT AND STUDENT EXCHANGES

Frank Schorn
Austin Community College, Texas

This chapter will describe two multiyear grant-funded projects designed to set up a framework for moving students to and from the United States for study in technical areas. One project, inspired by the North American Trade Agreement (NAFTA), was developed to move students between the United States, Canada, and Mexico. The other project moves students between the United States and Europe, in this case, Germany and the Netherlands. Both projects were partially funded by the U.S. Department of Education, Fund for the Improvement of Postsecondary Education (FIPSE). Additional funding for the projects came from the private sector and from our foreign college partners and their governments.

Introduction

Many community colleges have set up study-abroad programs that provide for a one-way flow of students from the United States to a variety of programs overseas. This chapter discusses setting up a program to send students abroad while allowing a flow in the other direction, that is, from the overseas site to the United States in what amounts to a student exchange program. These exchanges were directed at students in technical and occupational programs, not at students in liberal arts, where we traditionally find college exchange programs. In both projects, education and training helped prepare students from all countries to work in technical areas that exhibited a growing demand for labor. These included engineering technology and business, semiconductor manufacturing, metal-technology manual machining, computer numeric control machining, and laser technology. Two important program elements were the establishment of internships for students and the articulation of curriculum between colleges. The very difficult process of matching highly technical curricula provided an excellent opportunity for faculty to reexamine what they had been doing in their own courses. Subsequently, this process had widespread spin-off benefits that extended beyond the narrow confines of the initial project.

Austin Community College (ACC), in Austin, Texas, has six campuses and an enrollment of more than 30,000 students. Its Center for International Programs develops innovative international workforce training activities. The area around ACC is home to SEMATECH, a national consortium of semiconductor firms including AMD, Digital, Hewlett-Packard, IBM, National Semiconductor, Motorola, Texas Instruments, and Rockwell Semiconductor. Through SEMATECH, the semiconductor industry has developed a well-regarded curriculum for community and technical colleges to prepare students to qualify as semiconductor manufacturing technicians. ACC has been a leader in developing this curriculum, but the curriculum does not include any substantial work-based learning. The projects described below were structured to provide such a learning experience.

In designing a project, each college needs to consider its own strengths and weaknesses and come up with a proposal that fits its needs and the training needs identified in its region. Furthermore, the international partners will have their own needs and desires. Governments from a number of countries believe that the kind of student mobility this chapter describes is important, and they have put up the funds to take on the difficult task of making it happen. We believe that community colleges are in a strong position to be recipients of these funds.

Computerized Processes in Enterprises Involving Emerging High-Technology Occupations (COMPRO)

Introduction

This project was funded in 1999 by FIPSE under its EC/US Joint Consortia Program. It provided $180,000 for a three-year period; the European side provided matching funds. Under this program, partners in the United States and the European Community must submit identical proposals. The process of developing a joint proposal with an institution overseas is a good exercise in cooperation that pays off for all parties once the proposal is funded. This project established a multinational college-accredited set of student exchanges that included both work-based and school-based learning designed to prepare workers for technical jobs in industry.

The early phases of the project were spent meeting with our partners abroad to establish a framework for student exchanges that would be carried over after the grant funds were spent. The importance of developing a well-articulated vision for sustainability was instrumental to the success of the project and was emphasized in the grant proposal.

The narrative of the proposal submitted to FIPSE stressed that the need for a well-trained workforce in technical fields is critical to the future of every industrialized country. We looked for partners in the United States and Europe who had the same needs. In its search for European partners, ACC leveraged the partnerships already established in the Austin area, most notably the active sister city relations established in 1989 between Austin and Koblenz, Germany. Besides ACC, the other partners included the Maine Technical College System and Tarrant County College District in the United States, King William I College in Holland, and the Handwerkskammer Koblenz and the Dresden Chamber of Industry and Commerce in Germany. The Maricopa Advanced Technology Education Center in Arizona assisted in staff development for the project. AMD, Motorola, and the other high-technology firms provided support as business and industry partners. The grant proposal specified the role that each of the partners would play in the project.

ACC was the lead college in the United States for this project. All of the U.S. colleges involved sought to find new ways to send their students overseas for practical training and for international experience that would enhance their classroom experience. It was agreed that the best model for such programs would be one that kept students on track for their U.S. degrees. This meant that the coordination of curriculum was a vital objective for the U.S. partners.

Our European partners had slightly different objectives. In Europe, internships and work-based learning have a long history and are a firmly established part of the educational system. European colleges are constantly looking for new outlets for their students anywhere in the world. This project fit this need very well, and the U.S. partners benefited greatly from their years of experience in sending students overseas for practical work-based learning.

Project Design and Outcomes

The program, developed for students and faculty from both sides of the Atlantic, included the following elements. First, the curriculum design was built upon the entering technical knowledge of the students and allowed the full transfer of credit for the work completed at the overseas site. Second, supervised work placement (internships) brought classroom knowledge into practice. Third, a short-term program on language and culture improved the quality of the learning experience. Fourth, a program for recruiting students to participate in the exchanges was included. Fifth, a MATEC program for faculty development and for the use of instructional technology, including distance learning, completed the elements of the program. The details of each program developed under this project are numerous; here is a short list of the target outcomes over a three-year period:

- To sponsor learning exchanges for at least 45 students among the various partners

- To provide for full transfer of credit for education/training acquired abroad and offer the opportunity for students to stay on track for an associate degree
- To provide for replication of the project, making use of the sister city international network as one of the dissemination mechanisms
- To share information among the partners about instructional approaches, most especially those related to work-based learning
- To establish an international collaboration of educators and firms to prepare manufacturing technicians for targeted high-tech industries
- To document the activities of the project, including both successes and failures, in published materials

Here is a brief example taken from the report on one of the outcomes. In the first year, innovative high-technology work-study programs were designed in collaboration with our European partners and resulted in the placement of eight U.S. students. Progress was made that year in developing the curricular goals of the consortium by providing learning objectives and outcomes for the student internships. In Holland, this was in the area of semiconductor manufacturing in consultation with King William I and Phillips Electronics. In Germany, these included metal-technology manual machining, computer numeric control (CNC) machining, and laser technology in collaboration with the Handwerkskammer and local industry in Koblenz. European instructors were able to document the acquisition of specific professional competencies as well as identify international skill standards.

To add value to this experience, the students were asked to submit a final report, which included a general description of the work performed during the internship as well as a summary of the specific competencies and skills acquired. Opportunities for systematic reflection by the students, as well as provision for ongoing e-mail interchange with the students' U.S. adviser, were built into the program.

In addition, two internship models were developed during the first year. In Holland, students spent most of their time in a work-based three-month learning experience developed in conjunction with our training partner and with local industry. In Germany, students spent most of their two-month stay in formal instruction augmented by visits to local business and industry. Finally, representatives from project colleges participated in a workshop sponsored by MATEC, which outlined the CD-ROM curriculum design for faculty development on such topics as gowning for the clean room and semiconductor transistors. Participants learned how to best incorporate these materials into their classroom. This approach helped ensure projectwide familiarity with a standard set of training materials. Those readers interested in more details may consult the progress reports found on the ACC Web site, www.austin.cc.tx.us.

Major Challenges

We were able to accomplish the tasks originally set down by the project proposal, but not always in the way we had first anticipated. In particular, with such a complex multinational project, we found that the time it took to design and implement what we had agreed on was longer than we expected. Other, more specific examples are discussed briefly below.

First, because of the highly structured nature of the German educational system, it was difficult to articulate the curriculum between the partners. The model that finally evolved combined a mix of work-based and school-based customized instruction at a training facility, combined with visits to local business and industry. After some time we were able to integrate this learning experience so that it would strengthen each student's professional credentials.

Second, recruiting U.S. students to study in Europe was more difficult than finding European students who wanted to study in the United States. Although stipend money was paid from the grant to offset the additional costs incurred by students traveling and living abroad, the task of enlisting them was nonetheless difficult. In phase one, a total of 8 students from two U.S. colleges were placed in Germany and the Netherlands. In phase two, 14 students were placed, but 13 of them came from Europe to the United States, and only one went the other way.

Third, it was difficult to design equivalent exchange programs given the diverse training facilities within our consortium. In terms of the length and scope of the exchange experience, U.S. partners were able to arrange a two- or three-month study-abroad experience for their students. Our Dutch partner was able to provide a similar experience for their student in the United States. Given time constraints, as well as the nature of the German education system, however, our German partner in Koblenz was only able to arrange to have 10 master metal-technology instructors spend a month in Austin.

Fourth, designing the language and culture component posed problems. The program was constructed to improve the quality of the learning experience. The participating institutions were responsible for ensuring that the cultural and linguistic instruction necessary for a successful study-abroad experience was provided to participating students before, during, and after their study-abroad period. For U.S. students, language preparation included both conversational German as well as technical vocabulary building related to each student's industry focus. Our Dutch partner was particularly innovative in developing a program called "How to Survive in Holland."

During the first year, courses in conversational German introduced students to the spoken language, and intermediate German was customized for the welding technology students to improve vocabulary through participation and dialogue that used 350 specific occupational terms. The class was conducted primarily in the welding lab, which allowed the students to learn tools and processes through demonstration. Participants indicated that more time is needed for meaningful language application. From this experience, we have developed a wide range of materials related to cultural immersion.

Fifth, our partners changed over the life of the project. The original proposal included a corporate partner from Greece, but they decided not to participate. Later, the Handwerkskammer Koblenz informed us that the Dresden Chamber of Industry and Commerce was unable to continue to participate because of reorganization and resource constraints, and they informed the European Commission that the Handwerkskammer Luxembourg would become the new partner. We learned that because partners may change in a project that runs over several years, it is essential to have a design that is flexible enough to accommodate these changes.

The most important lesson we learned was that establishing strong professional and social links with the people we were working with helped us overcome most of the unforeseen difficulties we faced. Ideally, these links would be established before the start of the project.

Evaluation

Our evaluative methodologies included both predeparture and upon-return analysis through surveys, focus groups, interviews, debriefing meetings, and reports. These included the Interactive Qualitative Analysis (IQA), which consisted of a series of focus groups and interviews that produced systems-influence diagrams of the students' perceived value of learning in the exchanges. The elements of the predeparture learning system diagram included the technical training, language classes, logistics, social preparation, prerequisites, and unknowns about the school and living arrangements.

One major source of significant work-based learning for the students was the tangible result of an International Organization for Standardization (ISO) certification award. The students' participation in the German "dual system" differed considerably from what they were used to in the United States. From their experience, we learned that a beginning language class would be more helpful in learning a workplace skill than a specialized class in terminology. We found that students did acquire the language they needed out of necessity; however, for the students to fully participate and not merely observe the world around them, they required a greater command of the language. A description of the students' experience in another country's culture underscores the need for the bigger picture of global awareness and understanding.

The evaluation that followed the first phase included a greater documentation of skill standards and competencies obtained during the exchange program. In addition, student expectations, instructional staff attitudes, and industry perceptions were examined. The project evaluation has considered that this is an exchange program devoted to improving workforce preparation rather than an exchange between traditional university academic degree programs. It is based on the premise that to be successful and sustainable beyond the initial three-year period of the seed money funding from FIPSE, the COMPRO program must meet the needs of all participants in the project, especially industry partners, community colleges, and the students.

Technology for Industry through Mobility in Educational Sectors (TIMES)

Introduction

The second FIPSE project involving Austin Community College (ACC) is still in progress. The project was funded for four years with a $215,397 grant under the Program for North American Mobility in Higher Education. This program is run cooperatively by the governments of the United States, Canada, and Mexico. Its purpose is to promote a student-centered North American dimension to education and training in a wide range of academic and professional disciplines. The program funds collaborative efforts in the form of consortia, which must include at least two academic institutions from each of the three countries. Since the first grants were awarded in 1995, the time period for carrying out the activities has been extended from three to four years. The extra year was added so that colleges could devote the first year to setting up the administrative structure that would run the project before attempting to send students abroad for study. This approach underscores our own experience in the COMPRO (European) project, which showed that grant proposals tend to underestimate the time it takes to establish these exchanges.

Partners

The lead college in the United States is Austin Community College. The other U.S. partner is Mercer County Community College in New Jersey. For this project, Mercer will provide leadership in the development of curriculum, staff training, and the implementation of an international business model called the International Business Practice Firm. This model infuses international business skills and experiences into community college curricula using virtual simulations from different countries. The project currently involves practice firms in more than 20 colleges in the United States.

The lead college for Canada is St. Clair College of Applied Arts and Technology, located in Windsor, Ontario. It is centered in the industrial heartland of Canada, which has the largest concentration of tool and die/mold shops and auto-parts plants in the country. St. Clair's Canadian partner is the University College of the Cariboo (UCC), located in central British Columbia.

The lead Mexican college is Universidad Tecnológica de Coahuila in Saltillo. It brings to the project a well-developed automation program and an established method for course evaluation and modification that meets the needs of industry. Its Mexican partner is Universidad de Tecnológico de Tula-Tepeji, which has an excellent center for electronics training.

It is worth noting that the partnerships developed for the project had an early start with Sister Cities International. Austin, Windsor, and Saltillo are sister cities. Just as we were able to leverage these connections in the COMPRO project described earlier, so were we able to do the same for the TIMES project. Both ACC and St. Clair are members of CCID and were able to connect with each other through one of the networking opportunities afforded by CCID. A further discussion of the CCID network and some of its projects can be found in chapter 6.

Project Design

The purpose and design of this project are similar to those of the COMPRO project. It focuses on the exchange of students between the partners in the areas of engineering, technology, and business.

The project is designed to break down the barriers to student mobility among the NAFTA countries. It will do so by articulating courses among the partner colleges and by establishing a core curriculum that can be transferred to other colleges in the NAFTA region. As such, the project will set up a framework for student exchanges that can be used and replicated by the partners in the future. The exchange of students will at first be small. The project promises only that a minimum of 39 students (16 Canadian, 16 American, and 7 Mexican) will take part in the project, although many more faculty members will also receive training during the four-year life of the grant.

The key technology areas for articulation will be automation, computer technology, electronics and mechanical engineering, and international business. Exchanges will range from one to two semesters (long-term exchanges) to less than a semester for shorter intensive programs of study such as international business. For the technology areas, the project will use methodologies developed by the ISO

INTERNATIONALIZING THE COMMUNITY COLLEGE

to set the international standards for articulated curriculum. Students' competence will be assessed using Word Keys, a system that will assess the competence of all participating students in a consistent manner and will provide a method to link student competencies to occupational skill profiles in the related areas of study.

An integrating feature of all of the exchange programs is the inclusion of an online course, "Celebrating Cultural Diversity." This course will be required for all students engaged in the long-term exchanges and will be strongly recommended for shorter-term business exchanges. This course will provide training in language and culture, with a mix of music, arts and crafts, history, sports and entertainment, government, and political and social customs. The course will be offered for credit at all six partner colleges and will be available to other interested students outside of the project.

As with the COMPRO project, each college is responsible for ensuring that its students receive the required language and culture training before the exchanges occur. This means that students would ideally be identified a year before the exchanges took place, not an easy thing to do in the highly mobile student population of U.S. community colleges. In summary, the overall objectives of the project are the following:

- Align the core curriculum of the partner colleges through articulation agreements. This approach will include traditional classroom work, student internships, cooperative education, and field placements within industry. The goal is to provide a seamless transfer of credits without loss of time toward the degree.
- Establish a template for the articulation of a core curriculum using ISO methodologies. This template will allow the framework for exchanges to be exported to other colleges within NAFTA and will allow the impact of this project to continue beyond the project's funded time.
- Develop credit courses in international business that provide students with an opportunity to acquire solid international business competencies integrated with the essential workplace "soft skills." These courses will provide student-team-oriented business experiences, rich with technology.
- Formalize an agreement among all consortium partners regarding their financial commitment to the project and sustainability beyond the funding period, student recruitment and selection, student language preparation, student tuition and fees, student transfer of credit, and faculty and curricular development. This agreement was completed during the first year of the project.

- Develop an online credit course, "Celebrating Cultural Diversity." This course will not only provide training for the students engaged in the NAFTA exchanges but will also allow colleges to establish virtual exchanges.
- Develop and publish on the Web a manual for successful student mobility. The manual will include the process for student recruitment and selection, predeparture orientation activities, orientation and reception activities at the receiving institution, and integrating activities for returning students.
- Extend the articulation, where possible, to partner institutions within NAFTA, thus creating a multiplier effect.
- Produce an annual report on technology and business partners in the three NAFTA countries. The report will summarize students' experiences based on their observations of the differences and similarities in technology and business culture among the NAFTA countries.
- Develop innovative electronic connections among the consortium institutions. This will include the Internet, video teleconferencing, and other distance learning methods.
- Develop linkages with business and industry that can be used by students for practical experience or internships, cooperative education, and field placements. This will promote cooperation between business and industry and educational institutions and increase the pool of qualified skilled workers for NAFTA countries.

Conclusion

The multinational exchange program described in this chapter includes integrated work-based and school-based learning that prepares students for computer-related technical jobs and facilitates the portability of credentials. Both projects facilitated the exchange of students for a comprehensive internship experience. In total, our partnerships included at least nine institutions from Canada, the United States, Mexico, Germany, and Holland. The major purpose of the partnerships was to develop a more highly skilled labor force that is better able to understand the needs of the global market.

Articulating curriculum among countries is difficult and takes time. Our projects are complex and do not always work the way they were originally conceived; however, we need to remember that faculty and students are the main beneficiaries. The FIPSE grants for student mobility seem to be a perfect fit for the community college with their links to both colleges and business and industry. More colleges need to take advantage of these opportunities.

CHAPTER 8

PARTNERSHIPS ABROAD: INTERNATIONAL AFFILIATES AND FACULTY DEVELOPMENT

William Greene, Broward Community College, Florida
Robert Vitale, Miami-Dade Community College, Florida

Once a community college has explored ways to internationalize the curriculum and has initiated some study-abroad programs, it may be ready to pursue more advanced international education programs. Establishing linkages with institutions overseas and assisting them in developing an American-style curriculum can be very rewarding for both the U.S. college and the foreign partner. Such linkages not only promote access to American higher education in other countries but also provide significant opportunities to involve faculty and administrators in international education projects.

Community colleges are important providers of higher education opportunities for international students. *Open Doors 2000* reported that 17 percent of international students enrolling in U.S. colleges choose two-year institutions (Davis 2000). A 1996 survey (Chase and Mahoney) by the American Association of Community Colleges found that more than three-quarters of two-year colleges who responded had international student and immigrant enrollments, and that the total number of international, immigrant, and legal residents attending U.S. community colleges was more than 250,000.

While the attraction of U.S. higher education remains strong, there is growing resistance overseas to the cost of attending colleges and universities in the United States. The expense of attending a U.S. institution for four or more years is substantial for foreign students and their families as well as for sponsoring governments. Estimates of the cost for a year of study in the United States range from a low of approximately $18,000 in Mississippi to a high of approximately $44,000 in Massachusetts, and the total combined impact on the U.S. economy exceeds $12.3 billion (Davis 2000). In strictly economic terms, overseas education is an import for a student's country of origin, and large numbers of citizens studying abroad adversely affect a nation's balance of payments. Moreover, families in other countries are often concerned about the possible effects that four years of living and studying in the United States might have on the social, political, and cultural attitudes of college-age students. For these reasons and others, a growing number of U.S.-style college programs have been developed in several countries to enable students to complete some or all of their U.S. degree requirements at home, thereby reducing the time spent in the United States.

As community and junior colleges in the United States have pioneered the university-parallel two-year transfer model, it is logical that they would become active in establishing U.S.-style two-year college programs in overseas locations. When properly developed and structured, such programs can enable foreign students to complete up to two years of college-level work in their home country or region before transferring to colleges and universities in the United States. The advantages of this approach are many and obvious, and increasing numbers of international students are taking advantage of such opportunities. This is especially true for middle-class students from developing countries, where a college degree from a developed country is highly coveted. If U.S. colleges and universities do not provide sufficient opportunities, these students will seek out higher education systems in other countries. British and Australian universities are particularly aggressive in this market.

American higher education programs abroad are structured in several different ways. Some have loose or informal associations with U.S. colleges and universities, while others have established more formal linkages or affiliations. Several credit-bearing programs abroad have been established as branch campuses of U.S. institutions. The University of Maryland's University College has been offering higher education for U.S. military personnel overseas since 1949; in 1997, courses were offered in 27 countries and two U.S. territories (Rubin 1997). Most U.S. colleges collaborating with institutions overseas provide curriculum assistance and guidelines for academic standards. Several programs abroad use the course numbers, course titles, and catalog descriptions of their U.S. partners. Some American colleges operating abroad, such as Franklin College in Switzerland, the American University of Paris, the American University of Rome, and the American University in Cairo, have achieved full U.S. accreditation. Overseas programs linked with U.S. colleges usually make reference to their relationship in catalogs and brochures and on their transcripts. In branch-campus operations, the U.S.-sponsoring college usually issues an official transcript for students enrolled in the credit-bearing program abroad.

Broward and Miami-Dade International Affiliates

Broward Community College (BCC) enrolls more than 55,000 students on four campuses in the greater Fort Lauderdale, Florida, area. Miami-Dade Community College (MDCC) serves nearly 70,000 students on six campuses in Miami-Dade County. Both colleges offer university-parallel and technical/occupational programs.

Both colleges are members of the College Consortium for International Studies (CCIS), which allows member colleges to have access to the BCC and MDCC study-abroad programs.

Broward Community College has developed a comprehensive international education program and has been very active in establishing linkages with U.S.-style college programs overseas. Included in the Broward purpose statement is a strong international education component (BCC 2000, 22–23). BCC administers an overseas center for year-round study in Seville, Spain, and has conducted summer and short-term study-abroad programs for more than 25 years. BCC is one of only a few colleges in the United States to have an international general education degree requirement. Since 1974, BCC has conducted international education programs in more than 50 countries on six continents.

MDCC serves the traditional international areas of foreign languages and English-as-a-second language (ESL) instruction. In addition, the college administers study-abroad centers in Austria, Costa Rica, and France, and offers several faculty-led study-abroad options. International students from more than 90 countries currently attend the college's ESL and international student programs, which are among the largest and best known in the United States.

Broward and Miami-Dade have been actively involved for nearly 20 years in establishing linkages with American-style colleges and centers operating outside the United States and have pioneered the international affiliation model. Broward's first international affiliation agreements were signed in the early 1980s with colleges in Seville, Spain, and Kuala Lumpur, Malaysia. In 2000–01, several Broward and Miami-Dade international affiliation agreements were in effect:

Broward Community College
- Center for American Education—Singapore (Effective Date of Agreement—1986)
- Centre for American Education—Dubai, United Arab Emirates (Effective Date of Agreement—1991)
- Pan American Center for Higher Education—Cuenca, Ecuador (Effective Date of Agreement—1996)
- Van Hien University—Ho Chi Minh City, Vietnam (Effective Date of Agreement—2000)

Miami-Dade Community College
- American International College of Mexico—Mexico City (Effective Date of Agreement—1992)

Each affiliation agreement has been approved by the BCC or MDCC board of trustees, and each overseas affiliate is legally established to operate in the particular country where it is located. All affiliates are private institutions offering the first two years of U.S. university-parallel curriculum, although some offer third- and fourth-year programs in cooperation with other U.S. universities. Some also offer ESL courses and serve as testing centers. The language of instruction is primarily English at all affiliates.

All Broward and Miami-Dade international academic affiliations are similar. Each college provides technical assistance to the overseas institutions in the form of consulting services and curriculum materials. The affiliates adopt BCC's and MDCC's admission requirements and academic standards. Affiliate colleges are provided with, and are required to use, BCC/MDCC course numbers and titles, catalog descriptions, and course outlines. Affiliates are required to recruit and appoint faculty who meet criteria as established by Broward and Miami-Dade's accrediting association. Affiliates use textbooks and evaluation methods that are the same as or equivalent to those used in Florida. Broward and Miami-Dade teams, composed of faculty members and administrators, conduct regular visits to all international affiliates, usually on a semester basis, to monitor the parallelism and quality of the academic programs. The affiliation programs are supervised and administered at both colleges by full-time directors of international education. Additionally, faculty members or administrators are usually assigned to coordinate each affiliation. The intent is to assist affiliate colleges and centers in offering a quality U.S. higher education experience in the overseas location at reasonable cost. All expenses associated with international affiliate programs are borne by the overseas partner. No public funds are used by BCC or MDCC to support these programs.

Affiliates issue their own transcripts, clearly identifying the name and location of the overseas institution. A statement is included on these transcripts that the institution is academically affiliated with Broward or Miami-Dade. Neither Broward nor Miami-Dade represents that affiliate colleges share in its accreditation. Every effort is made to communicate to students accurate information regarding transfer options; all students attending Broward or Miami-Dade affiliates are provided with a transfer policy statement that clearly describes the transfer process.

In 1997, the BCC affiliation agreement with the Centre for American Education (CAE) in Dubai was revised to allow for extension centers in the South Asian region. New programs opened in 1997 include the Centre for American Education in Bangalore, India, and the American College of Higher Education in Sri Lanka. These institutions also offer the Broward curriculum and are affiliated with Broward through the CAE in Dubai, United Arab Emirates.

Broward's Singapore affiliation underwent a major enhancement during 1996–97. Broward received approval from the Florida State Board of Community Colleges and the Southern Association of Colleges and Schools (SACS) to offer an accredited program in Singapore under a Contract for Instructional Services with its affiliate, the Center for American Education. Eligible students attending CAE are admitted to BCC and receive official BCC transcripts reflecting the course work completed. This is the first instance in which Broward has moved beyond the affiliation model and established a credit-bearing branch-campus program abroad. The center also houses the United States Educational Information Center, the official U.S. government–designated office for advising Singaporeans interested in studying in the United States.

The Miami-Dade affiliation with the American International College of Mexico (AMERICOM) operates in Mexico City and Querétaro as an integral program of the Universidad del Valle de México (UVM), Mexico's third-largest private university. UVM enjoys full accreditation from the Universidad Nacional Autónoma de México (UNAM), which is responsible for accrediting all Mexican private universities. In addition, the Mexican Secretaría de Educación Pública (SEP) required the UVM-AMERICOM program to be planned as part of UVM's *licenciatura* (Mexican four-year degree), as all degrees in Mexico must be written as four-year degrees. These UNAM and SEP program approvals allow those students who do not transfer to remain in Mexico and continue on for the Mexican four-year degree. Additionally, AMERICOM's founding was endorsed by the consulate general of Mexico in Miami as an important educational component of the North American Free Trade Agreement (NAFTA) and received additional endorsement from the Florida State Board of Community Colleges. Offering a university-parallel transfer program leading to the associate in arts degree, the college has to date graduated more than 180 students, about half of whom have transferred for upper-division work in the United States and Canada.

As with Broward's affiliates, all courses in Mexico are taught in English by a largely bilingual faculty meeting the criteria of SACS. Miami-Dade Community College provides academic support in the form of curriculum design and instructional planning and is responsible for academic oversight of the program. All courses use MDCC syllabi and recommended textbooks. AMERICOM is also exploring the possibility of adding Associate in Science degree programs to its curriculum.

The Four-Year Connection

Although the primary mission of Broward's and Miami-Dade's international affiliates is to provide course work that will enable students to transfer, after two years of study, to colleges and universities in the United States, the two colleges have been collaborating with other U.S. institutions to offer additional courses at the upper-division level that lead to a bachelor's degree. For several years, Florida Atlantic University (FAU) in Boca Raton, a member of the State University System of Florida, conducted junior- and senior-level courses for business students at the Centre for American Education in Dubai, and it collaborates with Broward in conducting the program in Cuenca. Students can complete three years of study in Ecuador and then transfer to FAU in Florida, completing the bachelor's degree in just one year. In 1996, Regents College (Excelsior College as of January 2001) of the University of the State of New York agreed to recognize the course work offered in Dubai under the auspices of BCC and FAU and began awarding bachelor's degrees to students meeting Regents/Excelsior College degree requirements, thereby allowing students unable to spend any time in the United States the opportunity to earn a four-year U.S. degree in-country. The Broward/FAU/Excelsior College program is also being offered at the Pan American Center for Higher Education in Cuenca, Ecuador, and will probably be implemented at the other locations. Miami-Dade and AMERICOM have, as with the Broward programs, initiated negotiations with Excelsior College to offer a full U.S. four-year degree program in Mexico to AMERICOM students.

Both Broward and Miami-Dade have been active in assisting educational institutions in Argentina seeking to establish U.S.-style community college programs. Under the auspices of the Florida Consortium for International Education, Broward and Miami-Dade provided technical assistance and consulting services to enable Mar del Plata Community College to become the first U.S.-style community college in Argentina. In 1995, Florida governor Lawton Chiles signed a declaration recognizing the educational initiatives of Broward and Miami-Dade in Argentina (Holcombe and Greene 1996).

Faculty Involvement and Cultural Challenges
An important dimension of these undertakings is the opportunity afforded BCC and MDCC personnel to become involved in international education. In both developmental and operational stages, faculty and administrators provide significant input in their areas of expertise.

Typically, experienced faculty members assist firsthand in the development and implementation of specific courses and programs for the institution abroad in subjects they have taught for a number of years on the home campus. They travel to the affiliate institutions abroad to work with their counterparts and to learn from them. To quote one professor, "We sometimes learn that they do it better than we do." Thus, there are professional dividends for U.S. faculty members as they gather new insights from transnational comparative educational experiences that can be imported and incorporated in courses on the home campus. For faculty, there is also the realization and satisfaction that they have contributed meaningfully to a pioneering effort in international education. Continued oversight of affiliate programs by BCC and MDCC personnel provides for quality control abroad. In addition, both institutions have kept their accrediting agency, SACS, fully informed about the programs.

During the nearly 20-year period that Broward Community College has been conducting international affiliation programs, more than 100 faculty members and administrators have traveled overseas and collaborated with counterparts at partner institutions. College officials not typically involved in international education programs, such as the registrar, librarians, and learning resource specialists, have participated. A Broward faculty member is appointed to coordinate each international affiliation, and this process ensures the involvement of many faculty members who might not otherwise become active in international education. Additionally, Broward makes it a practice to send each member of its board of trustees to visit at least one BCC international program during his or her four-year term; this process has been very successful in increasing board members' knowledge of and support for international education. While BCC representatives give freely of their expertise and talent, they benefit considerably by working in an international environment and interacting with colleagues abroad. This, in turn, contributes in a significant way to the internationalization of Broward Community College. All expenses associated with travel to international affiliate sites are paid by the overseas partners and not by BCC or MDCC.

The institutional partner abroad often determines the level of complexity and the length of time involved in the actual implementation of the program. For example, an American or international private secondary school with many years of experience in the target country will know and readily understand the U.S. credit system, contact/credit equivalencies, and faculty degree requirements. These types of institutions seeking to develop an American college program have a distinct advantage in that they are already somewhat familiar with the U.S. system of education. Indeed, faculty and administrators in these schools, and in the college-level affiliates, are often temporary or permanent American expatriates.

With a foreign university attempting to create a U.S.-style two-year college program, the opposite may be the case. While there may be American or local resident faculty or administrators working in these institutions who have had some experience in the United States, the predominant administrative and academic culture is that of the host country. The U.S. institution must provide the framework for a firm U.S.-style base, and it often encounters resistance. A delicate intercultural balance must be found, insisting on American standards for a U.S.-style program while respecting the foreign system.

Sometimes educational cultures collide and require diplomatic efforts to reach a resolution. For example, UVM and Mexican universities do not honor or issue grades of D, whereas in the United States many institutions will count credits earned with a D grade toward a degree. The institutions reached a compromise whereby the American transcript indicated that the Universidad del Valle de México would not accept AMERICOM grades of D for those students intending to continue in the Mexican degree program.

Conclusion

Two-year U.S. college programs abroad are working. Significant numbers of foreign students are completing up to half of their U.S.-equivalent course work in their home country or region and are transferring successfully to colleges and universities in the United States and around the world. These programs are expanding, in a meaningful way, access to U.S. higher education for foreign students, as many would not be able to afford the cost of attending a full four-year degree program in the United States. The international efforts of Broward Community College and Miami-Dade Community College are an important innovation in transnational education and can be replicated in many overseas locations. While four-year colleges and universities will almost certainly continue to dominate the process of offering U.S. higher education programs abroad, two-year community and junior colleges will also play an important role in exporting U.S. higher education.

Bibliography

Broward Community College. 2000. *2000–01 Catalog*. Fort Lauderdale, Fla.: Broward Community College.

Chase, Audree M., and James R. Mahoney, eds. 1996. *Global Awareness in Community Colleges: A Report of a National Survey*. Washington, D.C.: Community College Press, American Association of Community Colleges.

Davis, Todd M. 2000. *Open Doors 2000: Report on International Educational Exchange*. New York: Institute of International Education.

Holcombe, Willis, and William Greene. 1996. "Florida Community Colleges Argentina Project." *Community College Journal* 66 (February/March): 35–42.

Rubin, Amy. 1997. "All Around the World, U. of Maryland Offers Classes to U.S. Military Personnel." *Chronicle of Higher Education* (21 March): A55–A56.

CHAPTER 9

CURRICULUM DEVELOPMENT: USING FEDERAL GRANTS TO STRENGTHEN BUSINESS PROGRAMS AND ACTIVITIES

Edward Stoessel
Eastern Iowa Community College District

There is currently an explosion of interest from abroad in forming linkages with U.S. community colleges, particularly in the business arena. From the U.S. community college perspective, there is a growing acceptance, if not an imperative, to integrate an international dimension into the educational experience. The federal government, in line with its policy objectives, supports a variety of programs that fund these linkages. By understanding what is driving countries to seek partnerships with community colleges and by understanding the benefits to be reaped by community colleges in entering into such partnerships, one can seek out and craft successful grant applications that meet the compelling needs of the international partner, the community college, and the federal government.

Eastern Iowa Community College District (EICCD) is a multicollege district operating three community colleges. The three colleges offer a wide range of arts and sciences and vocational/technical programs. The district enrolls approximately 9,000 credit students and 50,000 community education students. This chapter will describe how EICCD used grants from three different federal agencies to work on business education projects in India, South Africa, Ukraine, and Namibia. The major impact of these projects on EICCD was on faculty development and the internationalization of the business curriculum. However, the impact was also felt on other disciplines and on the community.

Why International Institutions Seek Linkages with Community Colleges

Many countries, particularly in Asia, Africa, and Eastern Europe, are making the transition from regulated economies with centrally planned controls toward economic systems characterized by entrepreneurial, free-market capitalism. These transitions are profound, complex, and difficult, requiring new knowledge, new skills, and the restructuring of educational institutions. In their struggle to respond to this dramatically changed environment, educational institutions in many countries are seeking partnerships with U.S. community colleges.

There are at least three tasks facing these institutions that have been identified as areas in which U.S. community colleges can provide critical assistance. First, they must develop the capacity to educate a broad range of students on the general theory and practice of free-market, entrepreneurial capitalism. Second, they must develop new specialized courses and programs of study to meet a rapidly increasing demand for training in specialized business fields such as marketing, business management, and entrepreneurism. Third, as many countries move from a centrally planned educational system to a locally controlled system, individual educational institutions must develop the capacity to work with the local business community to design training programs that will produce a workforce with the skills and knowledge required by the local economy. Educational institutions in these countries have little experience or expertise in these three areas. Community colleges, however, not only have the needed economic and business expertise, but they also have emerged as the premier international model for providing access to education and training that meets the needs of local communities.

Why Community Colleges Seek International Partnerships

Many, if not most, community colleges would now agree that providing an education that incorporates a global perspective is within their mission. Using federal grants to establish linkages with institutions outside the borders of the United States is an effective and low-cost (sometimes no-cost) method to actualize this component of the college's mission. There are at least three broad global education objectives that community colleges can accomplish through projects funded by the federal government. First, undertaking such a project establishes that the college endorses and supports the value of global learning. Whether the project provides for faculty development, student exchanges, hosting international guests, or providing technical assistance, it acknowledges and supports in a tangible way the college's commitment to an international agenda. Second, federal grants can be used specifically to strengthen the international component of credit as well as noncredit business programs, such as international business workshops or customized training for local companies. Third, the community college can use federal grants to assist local companies to move beyond simply exploring the theory and practice of international business to actually engaging in international business. Federal grants can provide the resources for the community college to serve as a catalyst to create trade missions and catalog shows customized to the needs of local small and medium-size businesses.

Federal Government as a Partner

A number of policy interests of the federal government are served by linking community colleges with educational institutions around the world. Three federal departments that have an interest in the international business arena and are the most frequent funders of community college international grants are the U.S. Department of Education (www.ed.gov/offices/ope/programs/international.html), the U.S. Department of State (http://exchanges.state.gov), and the U.S. Agency for International Development (www.usaid.gov/about).

These three federal agencies have an established history of funding U.S. community college projects. Through a diligent search of other federal bureaus, offices, and agencies, it is possible to find additional federal funding sources to support components of a college's international business education agenda. Details on the sources of federal grants can be found in the last chapter of this book.

Creating a Viable Business Education Project

The task facing a U.S. community college in designing a grant is to identify very specific goals, objectives, and activities that enhance the programs of the community college, meet the needs of the developing partner institution(s), and are aligned with public policy needs as identified by the federal grantor. What follows is an overview of four federally funded international business projects that were obtained by EICCD.

> Project No. 1
> • *Project Title:* U.S.-India Business Partnership Program
> • *Federal Funding Source:* U.S. Department of Education, Business and International Education Program, Title VI-B
> • *Amount of Funding:* U.S. Department of Education = $147,423

Background

Eastern Iowa was just emerging from a serious economic dislocation when this grant was in preparation in 1995. The local economy had been built on two pillars—the agriculture industry and heavy equipment manufacturing. Both of these industries were suffering greatly. The economic downturn demonstrated to the industries of the area, and to the community as a whole, the dangers of a nondiversified, narrowly focused economic base. International trade had been identified as a key component in a new economic strategy for the area. This project, designed to introduce small and medium-size companies to international trade, was a natural extension of these local economic development efforts. The business community rallied around the project, and five local organizations became formal partners in the project. Those organizations were EICCD, the Small Business Development Center-Eastern Iowa Subcenter, the Small Business Development Center of Iowa, the Davenport Chamber of Commerce, and the Iowa-Illinois Trade Association. The project focused on providing services and creating international trade opportunities for 15 companies. Perhaps more important than the impact on the 15 companies, the project served as evidence that the community was taking steps to create a more positive economic future, since it provided an opportunity to "globalize" what were once thought to be local markets. It was envisioned that in the long term this effort would stem outmigration, create new job opportunities, and produce new economic opportunities.

Project Design

For many small and medium-size companies, a full-blown, comprehensive, long-term, high-profile international trade effort is nearly impossible and perhaps too risky to undertake. Many smaller companies have historically viewed international trade as too complex, too expensive, too time consuming, and too laden with barriers and hurdles. With this in mind, this project provided a step-by-step, trimmed down, action-oriented approach to international trade. The goal was to demonstrate that locally based small and medium-size companies, even with limited resources, can successfully engage in international trade.

From the college's perspective, a major feature of the project design was to ensure that its business faculty were intimately involved. The project provided for faculty to travel to India to make arrangements for the trade mission (year one) and actually participate in the trade mission (year two). While in India, faculty conducted interviews, gathered materials, and observed the culture and business environment to develop case-study and enrichment materials. The faculty also interacted with local participating companies to glean additional course-enrichment materials. Faculty used these experiences to add an international component to their courses.

An additional element of the design was the creation of four skill-based international business courses. The four courses were (1) Freight Forwarding/Documentation, (2) Cultural Awareness and Understanding, (3) International Finance and Insurance Instruments, and (4) International Market Research. The courses represent sets of specialized skills and knowledge needed by business and industry to carry out and support international business efforts. The local business community had prioritized a need for all of these educational offerings.

The project was structured around four goals and 10 objectives. The major project goals were as follows:

Goal 1: Enhance International Business Education Programs in the Eastern Iowa Community College District.

Objective 1: Offer four new credit courses.

Objective 2: Modularize the content of the four courses for delivery in various continuing education formats.

Objective 3: Enhance the international component of existing business courses by broadening the skills and experience of the faculty.

Goal 2: Expand the Capacity of the Business Community to Engage in International Business Activity.

Objective 1: Establish actual trading relationships between companies in India and 15 local companies.

Objective 2: Establish an infrastructure that will support continued expansion of trade between India and the local companies.

Goal 3: Provide for Connecting Activities between the College Business Education Program and the International Activities of the Local Business Community.

Objective 1: Integrate work-based learning experiences into the business education program of the college and provide for hands-on and real-world learning opportunities for college business students.

Objective 2: Allow the business community to capitalize upon specialized resources of the college to assist in its efforts to realize international business opportunities.

Goal 4: Disseminate and Build upon Project Activities and Outcomes to Sustain the U.S.-India Trading Relationship.

Objective 1: Write articles and make presentations to appropriate community college and business audiences regarding this project model and its outcomes.

Objective 2: Using the resources of the 15 Small Business Development Centers in Iowa, establish a statewide network to promote, sustain, and expand Iowa trade activity with India.

Objective 3: Using the resources of the 60-member Community Colleges for International Development organization, promote, sustain, and expand U.S. trade activity with India.

Key Project Impacts

Business Community. The project directly affected more than 50 local companies in Iowa in a number of ways. A catalog with product and marketing materials of local companies was assembled and personally distributed by project staff to trade offices in Delhi, Madras, Bombay, and Bangalore.

The signature activity for the project was a trade mission to India. It was organized in partnership with the Iowa Department of Economic Development, the business community, and EICCD. Six local companies participated in the mission. Prior to departure, each company, working with faculty and with the Small Business Development Center, developed a country-specific marketing plan, became familiar with the business customs in India, and prepared itself for the trip. The success of the trade mission exceeded expectations. At the end of the project, four of the six companies reported having completed at least one business transaction in India. Of the two other companies, one had a sale pending and the other reported having a representative in India with prospects for a deal.

Faculty. Four college faculty members were directly involved in this project. They observed local companies making international business contacts, exploring business opportunities, and consummating international business deals. Using the knowledge and experience they gained from the project, they developed four new international business courses and created four instructional modules. As a result of this project, hundreds of EICCD students have been exposed to an expanded global perspective through changes in the curriculum.

Resource Center for U.S.-India Business Partnerships
To ensure that the beneficial effects of the project will continue, a Resource Center for International Business was established. It contains publication and other resources on business in India, including a videotape, "How to Do Business in India"; modules for an international business curriculum; Indo–U.S. business Web sites; an International Trade Data Network; and contact information on U.S. and Indian companies.

> **Project No. 2**
> - *Project Title:* U.S.–South Africa Business Education Linkage Project
> - *Federal Funding Source:* U.S. Department of State, College and University Affiliations Program
> - *Amount of Funding:* U.S. Department of State = $119,920

Background
The previous project described eastern Iowa's need to diversify its economy and seek international markets. As part of the community's effort to address this issue, EICCD sought to increase the international literacy of students and to build the international business capacity of small and medium-size local businesses.

The needs of the eastern Iowa community were not dissimilar to those of Port Elizabeth, South Africa. South Africa was also adapting to a new economic reality, and South African academic institutions were being asked to help ease the historic, cultural, and economic transitions occurring in the country. An important element in that transformation process was the creation of business opportunities for people who had been disenfranchised from the economic mainstream. The Port Elizabeth campus of Vista University was asked to be involved in training current and future entrepreneurs. Through the project, the Port Elizabeth campus sought to (1) equip students with the international business/culture expertise required for them to be successful in the global economy, and (2) provide community outreach and business support services to strengthen the competitive position of locally based small and medium-size companies.

Project Design

This project had three broad goals, each supported by specific objectives. The project goals and objectives were as follows:

> **Goal 1: Enhance International Business and Culture Education Programs at the Eastern Iowa Community College District and Vista University.**
>
> *Objective 1:* Broaden the international experience of the faculty and develop seven new international business/culture modules for credit and noncredit delivery.
>
> *Objective 2:* Create two videos: "Business Culture in South Africa" and "Business Culture in the U.S."
>
> **Goal 2: Establish an Infrastructure That Will Support the Expansion and Sustainability of This Affiliation.**
>
> *Objective 1:* Establish advanced communication linkages between the Eastern Iowa Community College District and Vista University that will serve the immediate and long-term purposes of the affiliation.
>
> *Objective 2:* Develop a plan to encourage the establishment of trading relationships between local U.S. and South African companies.
>
> **Goal 3: Disseminate Project Results and Expand the Scope and Impact of the Project.**
>
> *Objective 1:* Write articles and make presentations to appropriate college and business audiences regarding this project model and its outcomes.
>
> *Objective 2:* Establish a network beyond eastern Iowa to promote academic exchange and bilateral international trade linkages.

Key Project Impacts

Over the course of the project, there were 10 U.S. faculty visits to Port Elizabeth, South Africa. Besides carrying out specific activities for the grant, faculty conducted class discussions, participated in community events, addressed civic groups, and interacted with students on social and academic levels. These faculty developed course modules for the following courses: Business Psychology, Introduction to Business, Micro Economics, Non-Western Cultures and Values, Principles of Sociology, and Cultural Anthropology. These modules typically took the form of case studies, lectures, and demonstrations.

With the cooperation of the City of Port Elizabeth, a video program, "Doing Business in the Eastern Cape," was adapted for use in Iowa. A variety of books, magazines, and other instructional materials on the business environment and culture of South Africa were obtained. These materials are available at the Small Business Development Center and the EICCD library.

The Eastern Iowa Small Business Development Center sponsored a workshop, "Doing Business in South Africa." As a result of interest generated by this workshop, EICCD helped organize a catalog trade show at the Port Elizabeth City Hall in which eight Iowa-area companies participated. Representatives from nine Port Elizabeth companies attended the show. The Eastern Iowa Small Business Development Center continues to serve as a spokesperson and coordinator of small business international trade activities with South Africa. The final project activity was to produce a research report on trade possibilities between companies in eastern Iowa and the Eastern Cape. This report highlights both the cultural and economic realities of doing business in South Africa.

> **Project No. 3**
> • *Project Title:* Community College Partnership with Drohobych
>   State Pedagogical University
> • *Federal Funding Source:* U.S. Department of State
> • *Amount of Funding:* U.S. Department of State = $185,325

Background

EICCD has had long-standing relationships with the city of Drohobych, Ukraine, and more recently developed a relationship specifically with the Drohobych State Pedagogical University (DSPU). Muscatine, Iowa, home of Muscatine Community College of EICCD, has a sister city relationship with Drohobych. An exchange of various community members and leaders has been going on since 1990. During this process, EICCD established a relationship with DSPU and began to explore ways the two institutions could work together for the benefit of both colleges.

As the institutions shared with each other their missions, goals, and aspirations, it became clear what form the project activities should take. These activities not only support the program goal of the U.S. Department of State in fostering freedom and democracy but also are consistent with the defined goals of both institutions, will continue to affect the lives of their students, and will more closely link the institutions not only with their local communities but also with the global community. At the time of this writing, the project is in progress.

Project Design

All of the project activities are designed to confer benefits on both parties. The primary benefits to EICCD are twofold. First, through the development of cross-national learning exercises, EICCD students will have the opportunity to interact in a meaningful way with students from Ukraine. For midwestern students, who have little or no experience interacting and working with people from other cultures, this cross-national experience will be a powerful learning tool. Second, all EICCD faculty who travel to Ukraine on this project will develop a learning module, based upon this experience, to be incorporated into at least one of the classes they regularly teach. Through this mechanism the international experience of the faculty is leveraged so that a part of that experience is shared with hundreds of EICCD students over a period of years.

DSPU is seeking to play a key role Ukraine's struggle to emerge as an economically strong, viable, democratic country. Through this project, DSPU will expand its capacity to educate citizens in the new skills and knowledge required for a successful transition. DSPU will (1) enhance its capacity to equip both "traditional" and adult students with management, supervision, and entrepreneurial skills; (2) create a model for the development of new programs that are responsive to the needs of the local community; (3) strengthen its capacity to respond to the training needs of business and industry through a continuing education component; (4) establish an ongoing faculty development process to strengthen faculty awareness of the use of technology in the classroom; and (5) broaden the international perspective of its students. To these ends, DSPU feels it is imperative that they form affiliations with universities and organizations in the Western world. These contacts will expand the role of the university in the development of the Ukraine. Project objectives and key activities are as follows:

Objective 1: Increase the use of the Internet as an educational tool for faculty and students.

Activity 1: Assist DSPU in developing the infrastructure to help students and faculty use the Internet.

Activity 2: Partner EICCD and DSPU faculty to develop activities that involve the teaming of U.S. and Ukrainian students in cross-national learning exercises via the Web.

Objective 2: Adapt the program development and evaluation model used at EICCD to create innovative, modularized business programs to serve the needs of traditional students and the retraining needs of adults in the Drohobych region.

Activity 1: Develop a modularized course in management and supervision.

Activity 2: Develop a modularized course in entrepreneurism.

Objective 3: Enhance the capacity of DSPU faculty to provide world-class education and training through an expanded program of faculty development.

Activity 1: Provide a series of workshops on the use of innovative classroom teaching strategies.

Activity 2: Work with faculty to implement the concepts of Continuous Quality Improvement in the classroom.

Activity 3: Lay the foundation for the establishment of an annual Great Teachers Workshop at DSPU.

Key Project Impacts

DSPU envisions the project as having particularly significant impacts upon the use of technology in the classroom, outreach to local business, and faculty development. The most important outcome for EICCD will be the establishment of cross-national, student-to-student collaborative learning exercises. It is this activity, coupled with the opportunities for faculty travel, that will substantially enhance international learning experiences available to EICCD students.

Project No. 4
- *Project Title:* An International Development Partnership: Higher Education Linkages with Namibia
- *Federal Funding Source:* U.S. Agency for International Development, Association Liaison Office for University Cooperation in Development
- *Amount of Funding:* USAID = $99,800

Background

The lead college for this project was Highline Community College, with EICCD serving as a partner institution. Highline Community College has had a rich history of involvement in South Africa, including personal contacts with the rector and administrative staff at the Polytechnic of Namibia. The project focused upon creating a center for entrepreneurial development at the Polytechnic of Namibia.

Project Design

The Polytechnic has its roots in a trio of South African apartheid institutions. In 1994, legislation redefined the Polytechnic, creating the present institution. The Polytechnic is seeking to break out of apartheid-era structures and contribute to Namibian development. To carry out its mission, the leadership recognized that it must build an entrepreneurial culture to provide an avenue for historically disadvantaged Namibians to succeed in local, regional, and international marketplaces.

The activities of this USAID-supported project center around two broad themes, outreach to the community and capacity building within the Polytechnic. The outreach component of the project involves identifying and prioritizing the training needs of the community and developing the infrastructure to respond to those needs. This component includes contract training for business, industry, and nongovernmental organizations (NGOs) and government, and the development of support services to small and micro-businesses.

The institutional capacity–building component of the project involves elements including: initiation of a Great Teachers Workshop; creation of mechanisms for administrative professional development; the introduction of new technologies and teaching strategies; and the strengthening of the business and resource development functions of the institution. The project will support more than 20 faculty exchanges throughout the three-year period of the grant.

Key Project Impacts

As of this writing, the project is completing its first year of operation. Detailed outcomes are not yet available. However, discussion with the project principals has produced the preliminary judgment that the benefits of this program will be enormous for Namibia's educational system, business and industry, and economic development. New paradigms and models will be developed to address access to education by disadvantaged youth; relevance of the curriculum to employability; outreach to the community; fiscal management; and human resource development. The grant-supported activities will be just as beneficial to the U.S. partners as they seek to internationalize campuses and curriculum. The latter will be enriched through the series of exchanges with Namibian faculty, staff, and administrators.

Conclusion

These examples represent three different funding sources and four types of federally funded business projects. In all cases the projects are responsive to the interests of U.S. community college partners, the interests of the international partner, and the policy initiatives of the federal government.

While these funding sources offer an excellent opportunity to internationalize the business faculty and curriculum, the impacts of these projects extend beyond the business department in two significant ways. First, the projects can incorporate the participation of faculty members from disciplines beyond the business arena. In the examples cited, participating faculty came not only from the business department but also from the departments of psychology (business psychology), humanities (non-Western culture and values), and sociology (cultural anthropology). In the Ukraine example, faculty from a range of disciplines will travel to that country to develop the Internet-based cross-national learning exercises. Besides providing opportunities for faculty, these projects also allow mid- and upper-level college managers an opportunity to travel abroad and share their expertise and experience, thus strengthening their support for other international activities.

Additionally, these projects lead to change through the development of spin-off activities with the international partners. In every example above—India, South Africa, Ukraine, and Namibia—additional projects were developed. Generally, the partnering institutions put considerable time and effort into the initial establishment of the relationship. With the success of the initial project, new ideas inevitably emerge to capitalize upon and expand the partnership. What starts as a business project may evolve into student exchanges, faculty study abroad, the provision of specific technical assistance, or a major effort to assist in the establishment of a community college system.

In recent years, funding for business education projects has become more readily available. These projects not only internationalize the business departments of the college but, perhaps more important, open doors to a wide range of opportunities to internationalize the college and the local community.

Resources

Web sites for the grant programs discussed in this chapter:
- U.S. Department of Education Official Web site:
  www.ed.gov/offices/ope/programs/international.html
- U.S. Department of State Official Web site:
  http://exchanges.state.gov
- U.S. Agency for International Development Official Web site:
  www.usaid.gov

CHAPTER 10

CURRICULUM DEVELOPMENT: AN INTERDISCIPLINARY AREA-STUDIES APPROACH

Fay Beauchamp
Community College of Philadelphia, Pennsylvania

To transform curriculum so that it embraces the world, faculty members need to become a cooperative community, challenging assumptions and values through intellect, imagination, and experience. Although faculty members always need to explore this ideal, they also need to provide clear arguments for internationalizing the curriculum so that they can motivate the administration and funding agencies to supply the necessary resources. This chapter examines an area-studies approach to changing the curriculum. Drawing on my more than 20 years of experience in creating new courses and programs at the Community College of Philadelphia (CCP), I focus on the importance of faculty development as a necessary first step in transforming the lives and perspectives of our students.

While colleges must provide a lasting commitment to international studies through their own budgets, what follows reflects my judgment that outside grants are essential to creating significant change. To community college faculty, grants provide a freedom from administrative fiat or the pressures of factions among colleagues. They also encourage the achievement of long-term goals under a timetable, provide familiarity with current scholarship, and confer prestige by publicizing events and project results.

The funding agencies that are most receptive to community colleges range from foreign governmental to private foundations; for example, the Japan Foundation, the Japan–United States Friendship Commission, and the Ford Foundation. The most important, in my view, is the U.S. government. I make this judgment for two reasons: First, the National Endowment for the Humanities (NEH) has provided the basis for curricular change at my college over the past 15 years; the ideas for faculty development seminars evolved from six NEH seminars at CCP between 1982 and 1993 and also from individual faculty travel to an equal number of national NEH institutes. NEH, for this long period of time, has also been highly supportive of other community college faculty initiatives. Second, the U.S. Department of Education is the greatest source of support for international education projects undertaken by community colleges. Community College of Philadelphia has received two Title VI grants for a total of four years at an average of $85,000 a year.[1] The first grant, from 1996 to 1998, focused on East Asia and Africa; the second grant, from 1998 to 2000, focused on South and Southeast Asia, with the second year devoted to the Caribbean and Latin America.

The organization, however, that led my colleagues and me specifically to the area-studies approach to curricular change was the Asian Studies Development Program (ASDP), a joint project of the federally funded East-West Center and the University of Hawaii. An outreach program for all categories of U.S. colleges, in 10 years ASDP has taken care to invite community college faculty to participate in summer seminars and field-study trips to China, Korea, Japan, and Southeast Asia. Many of ASDP's most active regional centers are at community colleges that regularly host four-day workshops and ASDP national conferences. Through these activities, community college faculty are encouraged to continue research, experiment with teaching new material, and publish articles reflecting on this work. While area studies is normally associated with junior- and senior-level programs at colleges and universities, these grants facilitated an area-studies approach to faculty development resulting in new material for freshman- and sophomore-level community college students.

Institutional Commitment

This heading is one of the criteria used in evaluating Title VI grants. Chronologically, establishing that commitment comes early in efforts made by the faculty and administration to effect change. An institution needs to provide a context to sustain grant-funded activities beyond the life of the grant. This commitment can be demonstrated through matching funds, on the theory that if the institution adds a budget line, it is serious in wanting change. But money does not cause students to seek out courses; in community colleges, graduation requirements and transfer agreements can be essential and provide evidence of strong institutional support.

---

1. My analysis of the program descriptions and project abstracts prepared by Christine Corey for Title VI-A programs for 1999 and 2000 reveals the following trends. During the two years, 59 projects were funded, for amounts generally between $60,000 and $85,000 per year for two years. Of these a total of 21 were for area studies rather than, for example, global environmental studies or simply international development studies. Of these, 9 focused on Asia, 6 on Africa, and 6 on Latin America. A total of six community colleges were given new grants. The percentage is increasing, and as a reader for Title VI-A grants in fall 2000, I conclude that this increase is a result of informal policy, since there is no explicit policy of giving extra points during review. There are relatively few community college submissions, and more would be welcomed.

An open process that determines general education requirements should broadly involve faculty and administration. Accrediting bodies, Middle States in our case, ensure a collegewide process of building consensus for major requirements. It is not enough to internationalize a few elective courses for only 20 or 30 students per year. The power of community colleges is that they reach tens of thousands of students per year, through general education programs. The broader the requirement, the greater the number of students reached.

If general education requirements for community colleges do not already have an international component, students may be induced to take particular courses to satisfy the requirements of transfer institutions. Most students at CCP who transfer to a four-year college transfer to Temple University. Temple has an Intellectual Heritage requirement for all students; therefore, we decided to devote one quarter of 101-102 courses, which receive Intellectual Heritage credit, to the study of a non-Western culture. These humanities courses are packed with students—and it is not because we are persuading each student by advertising or advising them of the merits of the course. While it is true that word of mouth is positive about the intrinsic pleasures of these courses, the interlocking requirements of our institution and a major receiving institution led to our introducing hundreds of students a year to international material.

If faculty members at other colleges feel they do not have the support for the types of requirements that we have at CCP, my advice is to start small and build a cadre of faculty who believe in such an approach. Faculty members might start by taking advantage of programs such as those of NEH and ASDP that bring together participants from a variety of colleges nationwide to workshops and seminars. A positive experience at a summer institute can not only make a colleague a staunch ally in seeking curricular reform, but also can give the person the knowledge of theories, texts, and scholars that will help make the home institution's own efforts substantive and successful. Changing a curriculum takes time, but a few effective allies can work wonders.

Goals for Grant Activities

I am convinced that our true goal is to develop a good learning experience for our students by creating an intellectual environment in which faculty and administration can unite in love of learning about different cultures and work to improve the future of peoples throughout the world. But all administrators and agencies want measurable outcomes. Whatever reading, research, discussion, and presentations faculty may engage in, community colleges want to see that teaching is directly affected in specified courses. There are two products that can be used to evaluate this impact: written course modules and new course descriptions.

Modules

The process of creating new modules is known as course infusion. In this process, an existing course is infused, or enriched, with new material to make it more appealing to student and teacher alike. When our World Literature 245 course at CCP started with Greek plays and Plato, veered through Machiavelli, and ended predictably with the tragic hero in *Hamlet* or *Macbeth,* I thought it was, if not dull, an example of the established canon taken neat. Once I added Murasaki's *Tale of Genji,* with its Chinese as well as Japanese sources in poetry and tale, the course fascinated me and led students to original insights comparing Shakespeare with an equally outstanding woman author. For our World Literature 246 or Humanities 102 courses, a unit on China and Japan was the only true way to explain the genesis of modernism—Ezra Pound, T. S. Eliot, and W. B. Yeats would not have created modern definitions of poetry without having read Fenollosa's manuscripts of Chinese poetry any more than Whistler, Monet, and van Gogh would have created the beginnings of modern art without having seen hundreds of woodblock prints of Hiroshige.

These references to literature and art come from my own examples of infusion modules. Over five years, about 60 of our faculty have produced modules with support from grants. In addition to English and interdisciplinary humanities courses, most modules have been created in philosophy/religion, world history, anthropology, art history, music history, and political science; interdisciplinary modules have also been used for linked reading and writing courses in English-as-a-second-language, developmental, and honors programs.

Modules are typically from 4 to 10 pages long and are used for two to four weeks of a course. The module itself cites readings and may include brief excerpts. The creative part consists of study/discussion questions, directions for small group work and other classroom activities, assignments for essays and longer papers, and test questions. The sequence of activities from informal writing through discussion to more formal assignments reflects much of the research done in the last 20 years on learning and writing. Although the teacher may add narrative that explains to other teachers how this section fits within the larger course or within a theory of the discipline, much of the package contains pages that can be copied and handed out to students. Such useful products encourage teachers to teach new material; through dissemination, many faculty find it easy to innovate by using the assignments.

New Courses

The second product we have used to evaluate the impact of grant activity is a detailed description of a new course. At my college, the standard model for requesting a new course includes the rationale, course framework (required elements), sample assignments, bibliography, sample syllabi, and evaluation techniques. Groups prepare these course description packets. For example, through our grant activity we have created five new interdisciplinary humanities courses in the cultures and civilizations of Japan, China, Africa, Latin America, and modern Asia/Africa; an anthropology course on the peoples of Asia; two English courses in Asian and African literature; and Japanese and Chinese language courses. While group work is slower than one individual writing the course, the group's discussions reveal different assumptions and different theories of the discipline as well as different areas of expertise. The course framework allows for enough variation so that different semesters can highlight different geographical subregions, periods, or themes. By having typically three syllabi in a course description packet, the range of choices that can meet the same criteria encourages future teachers to play to their strengths or to experiment. The course descriptions are formal documents that are used to achieve departmental and administrative approval of the courses, but they are, in fact, frequently recopied by teachers who want to use them as a source for new ideas.

Advantages of an Area-Studies Approach

Based on an evaluation of what we have achieved in five years, I am confident that the area-studies approach is highly effective for faculty development and the infusion of existing courses. But why should a college begin with faculty development using area-studies categories such as Southeast Asia or Africa instead of taking an approach based on a single theme, such as the environment or women's studies?

The answer is there are advantages in working with a traditional American academic division. Because of decades of area-studies development at universities, partly subsidized by Title VI grants, many departments are organized around a specific culture. For example, Japanese studies is not scattered among philosophy, history, and art departments, as it might be at a community college, but is the province of a number of specialists concentrated at one center. For the purpose of faculty development, then, community colleges can form alliances with these area-studies centers, as CCP has done with different National Resource Centers at the University of Pennsylvania. Columbia University, the University of Chicago, and the University of Hawaii are the three other notable universities that also have resource centers that work tirelessly with nonspecialist faculty, sending out scholars who travel and whose scholarship travels well also.

The Value of Interdisciplinary Study

Another advantage of an area-studies approach is that holding one location constant allows for variety in discipline. On the very simplest level, this interdisciplinary involvement is essential for significant curricular change: Quantitatively, more departments and more courses reach more students with different interests.

The area-studies approach can create a coherent process for curricular reform that can be extended over a number of years as a college's faculty studies one area after the other.

The connection between cross-cultural and interdisciplinary learning, however, is much more profound and interesting than just the number of students affected. Why is such breadth important in the first two years of any college, the two years that are the specialty of community colleges? As soon as the question is posed, one can see that students need to explore different disciplines and different cultures to determine their fields of study and to choose careers. Also, community college students are at a point in their lives where they will either enter the world of work or transfer. It is important that they understand how culture shapes the decision-making process and how different groups of people approach these decisions with different sets of assumptions and values. Where else will many of these students get this understanding, if not in introductory college courses?

The definition of culture includes the attitudes and values of a group of people; cultural study explores the geographical and historical reasons why one group of people has developed a set of traditions and beliefs. Academic disciplines themselves are full of cultural assumptions and traditions; juxtaposing disciplines makes students aware of basic principles, just as juxtaposing Chinese and Greek cultural attitudes or Nigerian and English attitudes makes students aware of untested assumptions. Using interdisciplinary and intercultural comparisons together makes each comparison a more powerful analytical tool, one that helps students become independent, curious learners.

Limits to an Area-Studies Approach at a Community College

While I am promoting an area-studies approach to faculty development, once courses are transformed, I am not recommending that they be isolated in different programs focused on Asia, Africa, or Latin America. My preferred approach would be to work on an institutional structure that sets up clusters of courses that will enable teachers in these various areas to continue planning and learning together and to encourage students to attend cocurricular activities centered on many different areas of the world. At this time we have a number of small programs such as the Honors Program, the Transfer Opportunities Program, and the Humanities Enrichment Program. Students in these programs receive an interdisciplinary/intercultural learning experience by block-scheduling a number of complementary courses that are team taught. We would like to expand these programs, which transcend area boundaries and juxtapose world cultures.

Organizing Faculty Activities

The process of organizing the faculty development activities financed by grants has many elements. Each college will have its own ideas about the mixture of lectures, workshops, seminars, and so forth, that is most appropriate to its needs and circumstances. What I would like to do here is comment briefly on some of the organizational matters we faced.

Outside Consultants

We built the services of an outside consultant into our grants to help us plan our faculty development activities. Having a paid outside consultant offers a wonderful opportunity for a community college generalist to work collaboratively with an established area-studies specialist. The community college project director brings expertise in pedagogy, administration, and, usually, one discipline. Ideally, consultants have not only published articles and books and been active in national organizations; they also have their own reasons for wanting to make international study more accessible to undergraduate students. For an interdisciplinary focus, one wants a scholar with an eclectic range of interests. These consultants suggest reading lists—editions or translations for primary texts and bibliographies for supplemental reading. They also suggest speakers and scholars able to work effectively with generalist faculty; to do so, consultants need to know individuals, not just books.

Good consultants not only help generalist faculty design and implement grants and effect curricular change; they also bridge the great divide between the research university and the community college. Respecting the different kinds of knowledge community college professionals have acquired in a lifetime of reading, teaching, and travel, consultants help faculty enjoy research and share their results on a national level.

Outside Scholars as Presenters

While all outside scholars play some of the roles of the consultant, other roles they take on go beyond what I have outlined already. When specialists come to a campus for two or three days they can spark wide interest in particular issues, authors, and texts. We have found that once they are away from their obligations at home, professors are remarkably generous with their time, for only a daily honorarium. Our set schedule has been to ask for a public lecture, with students as the key audience, for about two hours including questions and answers. The key to getting a large audience is to schedule the lecture during a class time and provide materials to encourage faculty to incorporate the topic in the course syllabi. The lecture is followed by a lunch with five or six faculty members and conversations that range, for example, from future predictions as to the viability of Pan-Africanism to advice on specific bibliographies. Finally, in a Teaching Center Workshop open to all faculty and staff in the afternoon, the scholar usually begins with an informal talk that presents an issue, a controversy, or a theoretical approach. We generally ask our faculty to read one article or book to prepare for the workshop; the ensuing discussion, often in question-and-answer form, focuses on the topic or reading, yet is relaxing for the visiting scholar.

A variant on this structure has two scholars complementing each other; there are advantages to juxtaposing viewpoints and organizing a bigger event to attract a larger student audience. In a day's activities, this format puts controversy into a historical perspective, revealing the assumptions and biases of those who argue about this subject. Another technique we have used is to invite scholars to give a miniconference on campus. One semester we had a two-day event beginning with a professor of ancient Egyptian art from New York University. His talk on symbolic iconography was followed by a lecture by a curator from the University of Pennsylvania archeological museum whose specialty was artifacts showing the relationships between ancient Nubia and Egypt. By having the two speakers in one day, we had a series of lectures that attracted more than 200 teachers and students who listened to a range of topics that were taught in more than a dozen courses. The next day we had speakers on Arabic literature and modern Egyptian history and literature.

Inside Consultants and Resources

In closing this section on using academics to lecture and lead discussions, I want to discuss the importance of weaving into the fabric the knowledge and experience of community college colleagues. At universities where research is a key element of professors' careers, using in-house expertise in interdisciplinary programs is an obvious strategy. The expertise of community college professors, however, is all too often undervalued. In the international realm, the caliber of research available from our own faculty has been a major strength in our endeavors. We have faculty with Ph.D.s from distinguished universities throughout the world. Ph.D.s or not, our colleagues from Thailand, the Philippines, India, and Congo have been major resources to us, as are our American-born faculty, with their wide variety of personal experience of foreign residence, research, teaching, and publication.

New programs are not only strengthened by the expertise of colleagues but can also benefit from using the existing infrastructure for faculty development. In our case we have the Community College of Philadelphia Foundation, the Teaching Center, and the Office of Student Activities, which we relied on for support.

Primary Texts as the Center of Workshops

All of our speakers, whether internal or external, were encouraged to center their presentations and discussions on specific texts. The core position of primary texts in interdisciplinary area studies has an interesting history in American higher education. There is no doubt that my own community college's reliance upon primary texts in course requirements, as well as in faculty development activities, stems from the NEH guidelines—dozens of our faculty leaders have been introduced to the methodology of discussing primary texts through NEH seminars. The idea of humanities is, of course, interdisciplinary, and I trace the creation of interdisciplinary humanities courses to the University of Chicago, which, 40 years ago, added courses on Indian and Chinese culture and civilization to its mix of humanities courses, which highlighted Greek texts. The University of Chicago has long had a Great Books tradition, in which groups of nonspecialists closely examine texts, asking a series of open-ended questions that honor ambiguity and alternate interpretations. Group discussion, rather than lectures, is used to encourage independent thought; freshmen are required to take these humanities courses to acquire analytical skills that are sensitive to the implications of words and skeptical of opinion dressed as fact. The goals of this pedagogy, therefore, are similar to the goals of interdisciplinary and multicultural work.

The University of Chicago also nurtured John Dewey as he developed ideas on the relationship of democracy and education; he believed that the scientific method underlay all learning. I add these thoughts on pedagogy because so much of what we do in our area-studies courses stems from Dewey. We don't develop courses based on a survey of centuries followed by multiple-choice tests; instead, we choose key texts to represent the whole. We design courses to put the student in the center of the learning process—observing, questioning, and testing hypotheses.

Running a Four- to Six-Week Seminar at the Community College

The challenge of faculty development on international topics is to achieve coherence. Colleges always have slide presentations, music and dance recitals, lectures, readings of poetry and fiction. What makes faculty development based on an area-studies approach distinctive is that each presentation or lecture builds upon the other and suggests different dimensions of the same topic. Project directors must design a contextual framework faculty members can use in their courses for a great variety of assigned texts. One way to create coherence is to design an intensive seminar that resembles graduate course work.

Our forte at CCP, honed through years of meeting NEH guidelines, is creating five-week seminars. Here are some basic elements: (1) from 18 to 25 participants are paid and are committed to coming prepared for the entire session;

(2) project directors act somewhat as panel chairs—introducing, timing, making transitions, and summarizing but not teaching; (3) required readings are chosen in advance and the books are ordered; (4) outside professors lead sessions for two or three days at a time; (5) sessions last for two hours in the morning and two hours in the afternoon, usually four days a week; (6) trips to museums and historical sites occur on the fifth day, and often evening outings to performances are scheduled as well; and (7) each participant produces a course module after the seminar is over but before receiving a final payment.

The seminars focus on a few geographical areas; in addition, chronology and themes provide coherence. This structure models the courses we design. An introductory course, such as one on African cultures and civilizations, will be narrowed by the individual instructor to two or three representative countries, a few periods, or a few themes.

The Language Component of Interdisciplinary Area Studies

For any Title VI grant, developing the foreign language curriculum is a vital component. At CCP, we were fortunate to begin our area-studies faculty development program with Japan and China, because the need for courses in Japanese and Chinese was very clear. We offered no courses in these languages in 1996; five years later we were adding a second year to both Japanese and Chinese language courses. The language teachers and the teachers of the culture and civilization courses work cooperatively, using, for example, examination of a poem or philosophical text with multiple translations to infuse language learning into the interdisciplinary culture and civilization course. But our greatest success in getting teachers and students to experiment with a foreign language across the curriculum (FLAC) model occurred the semester of the study-abroad workshop described in the next section. This trip motivated many nonlanguage faculty to develop materials in Spanish.

A Four-Day Experiential Workshop in Merida, Mexico

Our second Title VI grant ended with the Caribbean and Latin America. A unique project that evolved out of our grant-funded activity allowed 11 faculty members and 9 students to study briefly in the Yucatán. The four fully scheduled days in Merida were similar to four days of a faculty development seminar in that they combined lectures and discussions of specific texts. The ruins of Dzilbalchaltun and Uxmal, however, astonished both faculty and students who had only studied the sites through texts, prints, and slides. Visiting the city of Merida raises the question of which civilization assimilated the other; as a group we became increasingly aware of the contemporary Mayan presence in the food, clothing, art, and even hammocks.

I want to emphasize the interdisciplinary aspects of this amalgam of faculty development activity and cocurricular activity for students. A professor of Spanish had initiated the venture, but our trip was enriched by the perspectives of the other faculty members who went with us. Besides Spanish and English teachers, we had teachers of anthropology, art, music, and world history giving formal presentations in Mexico to our students. Field trips immediately illustrated the points made, in full color and complexity.

In a way, this workshop was an ultimate team-teaching, interdisciplinary area study. In their evaluations, the students spoke of their wonder in joining teachers as we all leapt from idea to idea, contradicting one another and then moving to resolution, asking questions, and, mostly, laughing and enjoying learning and experiencing a foreign culture.

Project Evaluations

Evaluation occurs on many levels. We have had regular evaluations with enumerated grids to judge outside speakers and our summer seminars. Students and faculty filled out extensive written evaluations of the Merida workshop with both quantitative and qualitative data. For each two-year project, we used an outside evaluator who met the faculty and read the course modules and new course description packets. We tracked a number of students and courses and gave students evaluations beyond those regularly required. Many of the issues and procedures that were relevant for these projects are the same as those for any of our teaching.

Dissemination of Area-Studies Research, Curricular, and Teaching Materials

Before describing the possibilities for dissemination of area-studies materials, I want to pause and make a case for the importance of writing, doing research, and attending conferences for the community college faculty member. A few months ago I was writing a new grant proposal for a project to help faculty who were not specialists in Japanese studies conduct and share research. A person at a research university, who read the grant at my request, opposed the emphasis on conference participation and publication because he thought modifying teaching in the classroom should be the sole focus of faculty development. His opposition was particularly relevant to community college faculty who are moving into an academic field where they have little or no graduate training.

At a university, a concern may be that professors do not care how scholarship is translated into better teaching; community college professors, however, face overwhelming opposition to doing anything other than teaching a maximum number of students. Yes, grants are funded to improve our teaching. Yes, products such as modules and new courses are essential to that goal. But teachers of the first two years of college, teachers of introductory courses, must be expected to have an intellectual life, to question assumptions, to make observations, to form hypotheses, and to seek evidence for opinions. How can we possibly be models to our students if we do not read primary texts and secondary scholarship ourselves? The workshops and seminars I have been describing only begin to prepare us for teaching cultures with which we have had little or no experience. Continuing individual research is essential to being a responsible professional at the community college. On a much simpler level, grants encourage dissemination of materials so that an investment in one teacher affects many teachers. For topics in area studies, there are many forums for this dissemination.

In-House Dissemination of Teaching Materials

I have described the production of teaching modules: with word processing and excellent duplication facilities, in-house publication is of professional quality. With more and more faculty having personal Web pages, technology is obviously revolutionizing dissemination. Since this process is not specific to international work, let me just say briefly that the route to sharing material regionally or nationally begins at home. Workshops that last an hour and a half give an individual teacher the opportunity to present material in a cultural context and then lead other teachers in a thorough discussion of a topic. At our Teaching Center we schedule three or four of these workshops a semester.

National and Regional Conferences

For approximately 20 years, the Community College Humanities Association (CCHA) has encouraged community college faculty to use innovation in teaching courses on different cultures. At their meetings, an individual or a panel of teachers can share new ideas about texts and contexts while learning about key authors and scholars and the best projects regardless of geographical area of interest.

In the past 10 years, along with the growth of community colleges themselves, many other organizations have become open to community college participation. I have mentioned the Asian Studies Development Program; ASDP has been organizing national meetings specifically so that generalists beginning to teach about Asia can share papers in a supportive context. In different years, four of my colleagues and I have traveled to China, Korea, and Japan on ASDP-sponsored field trips; five others have gone to three-week introductory seminars on Asia at the East-West Center in Hawaii. The 1997 ASDP Silk Road Trip across China to see the Buddhist art treasures of Dunhuang and the bazaars of Kashgar was my own ultimate faculty development activity. Almost all the participants have shared the products of this experience at successive national ASDP meetings.

ASDP meetings in the past have been held before meetings of the Association of Asian Studies (AAS); papers at AAS meetings are almost exclusively given by specialists with graduate training and knowledge of Asian languages. While community college faculty rarely give papers at national AAS meetings, attending them is important, both to learn more about the topics one teaches and to hear leading scholars one might want to bring to a community college campus. Regional meetings of AAS, on the other hand, welcome community college teachers as panelists. The Mid-Atlantic Regional Association of Asian Studies (MARAAS), for instance, welcomes research in relation to new teaching as well as research that extends the knowledge of a field.

Here I want to make special mention of the Japan Studies Association (JSA), which started as an organization for state colleges and universities and has increasingly welcomed community college faculty. Several community college people, including myself, are currently on its board. We all have contributed at yearly conferences of JSA and are currently designing a summer seminar for generalists with support from the Japan–United States Friendship Commission.

Publishing

There are many publications that seek contributions from community college faculty. The *CCHA Journal* frequently publishes articles on area-studies themes. *Teaching English at the Two-Year College* also gives careful feedback to all contributors. ASDP, JSA, and the regional AAS organizations publish yearly collections of conference papers that have been through a review process. *Hispanic Outlook* has a large circulation and has published a two-part article on the Mayan world summer institute organized by CCHA with NEH funding; it published an illustrated article on our Merida workshop in January 2002.

Conclusion

I attach great importance to faculty development as a way to integrate international and intercultural material into the curriculum. For 15 years after graduate school, I felt sustained at my community college by social commitment, connections with students, and the support of colleagues. The faculty development activities I have been describing, however, gave me a chance to work on a national level for social commitment to world peace and understanding. It has made meaningful all my experience with foreign lands that began when I was a child in occupied Japan. But perhaps more important to me was the fact that the work that began in an ASDP-organized NEH summer institute on Japan enormously enriched my intellectual life. Community colleges must be places that encourage their faculty, as well as their students, to pursue goals that produce such an outcome. We cannot be expected to inspire our students unless we have the energy that is the product of new perspectives on our changing world.

CHAPTER 11

SMALL PROJECTS THAT PROMOTE AN INTERNATIONAL CAMPUS CULTURE

Linda A. Korbel, American Council on International Intercultural Education, Oakton Community College, Illinois

Members of the higher education community frequently regard the process of internationalizing the college campus as somewhat mystifying and certainly costly. Administrators and faculty alike have tended to associate internationalization with large-scale initiatives requiring student and faculty mobility, dedicated facilities, and significant numbers of staff hours, all of which can amount to a major expenditure of resources, both financial and human. Yet over the past 20 years, as more and more community colleges have embraced the imperative to produce globally and multiculturally competent citizens, economic realities have forced them to become more creative in developing activities and programs that deliver high impact at low cost.

We only have to look at the statistics compiled each year by the Institute of International Education's *Open Doors* research study to see that just a fraction of U.S. college students are able to incorporate a direct international experience into their college program, fewer than 1 percent across the spectrum of higher education (Davis 2000). Community college students often face the special challenges of commitment to job and family responsibilities, as well as financial barriers, when they consider spending time in an international setting for study abroad, exchange, or workplace internship experiences. Therefore, the task of preparing students to be effective citizens of the globe becomes a domestic matter, related to curriculum, campus environment, and both co- and extracurricular programming.

The American Council on International Intercultural Education (ACIIE) has worked for more than 20 years with community colleges across the United States, as well as with similar institutions in other countries, to serve their information needs as they attempt to create such programs and activities that will benefit their students and their communities. ACIIE is an affiliate council of the American Association of Community Colleges (AACC), with a membership of approximately 120 colleges involved in international and intercultural education. ACIIE shares expertise and provides information on topics such as cultural diversity, multicultural relations, foreign student recruitment and exchanges, faculty exchanges, professional development programs, and funding opportunities for international and intercultural activities. ACIIE helps community colleges cultivate educational partnerships and participate in programs with organizations worldwide. ACIIE pursues this mission through annual conferences, a print newsletter for its membership, an e-mail subscription list and Web site, videoconferences, and other programs and activities that foster the dissemination of information and networking among members. For more information, visit the Web site, www.aciie.org.

Recognizing the keen interest in model programs, ACIIE is compiling a manual of best practices in global education for community colleges, scheduled for release in spring 2002. As executive director of ACIIE, I have thus had the opportunity to work with many community colleges and have learned of their successes firsthand.

The focus of this chapter is to present a representative sampling of their initiatives, with a special emphasis on those that can be easily replicated on other community college campuses. Our readers will no doubt recognize some of these models, as they may have already been implemented in some fashion at their own institution or at others they know. For many community colleges, the process of globalization began with the recruitment of international students and their integration into the life of the institution. The presence of this extraordinarily rich resource on a campus offers great potential for creating and expanding awareness of other cultures for all members of the college and the surrounding community.

Case Studies

The case studies that follow highlight some small-scale, low-cost methods that colleges have used to promote an international campus culture. The featured projects include special events, programs involving international students, staff development activities, minigrants, diversity training, student clubs, modifications to campus environment, technology-enhanced activities, and community outreach. Since several projects extend into more than one area (for example, special events that involve international students on campus), the cases have been organized by college rather than by category.

At **Kilgore College** in Texas, the international student program has grown from 2 students in 1990 to 118 in 2001, representing 37 different countries. During November, to celebrate the first nationally declared International Education Week, Kilgore capitalized on their presence by involving the students in a variety of activities, from tabletop displays of cultural artifacts and wearing traditional dress to presenting a Japanese tea ceremony and hosting traditional games for children. Kilgore invited civic groups, community leaders, and all of the K-12 schools in the area, in addition to their own students and staff. The events drew more than 500 people. On the second day, international students cooked dishes representative of their culture's cuisine for some 200 American students and community residents to sample. Later in the week, returning international students participated in a panel to share their experiences as students at Kilgore. Other students visited area universities to learn about transfer opportunities and also to participate in International Education Week activities on those campuses. The week ended with a party for these international students who had contributed so much to the celebration.

Harford Community College is a midsize college located in rural suburban Baltimore, Maryland. Since the mid-1990s, the college has become engaged in international and globalization initiatives, including partnerships with institutions in Russia, Morocco, and Germany. On campus, five simple and inexpensive enhancements to the campus environment reinforce the notion that Harford is part of a global community: International clocks purchased at minimal cost have been installed in the lobbies of five campus buildings to show local times in 30 cities around the world. At each installation, a short description has been provided to situate the viewer in relationship to the rest of the world. Here is one such text: "As you stand here at 1:00 p.m., a mother in Rio de Janeiro puts her baby down for a 2:00 nap. As you think about having lunch, late afternoon shoppers wander the souk in Casablanca, and the 8:00 curtain rises at the Bolshoi Ballet in Moscow. In Singapore, the next day has arrived." The walkway leading to the new student services building is lined with 25 flags, representing the countries of origin of students, faculty, and staff. Duplicates of these flags are used to decorate the dining rooms for the international luncheon held each fall. At the luncheon, international students, faculty, and staff are invited to share a few words in their native language or talk about their native land. In 1999, students voted to rename the campus restaurant facility the Global Café, where international murals grace the walls. And in the campus bookstore, the plastic bags for purchases are imprinted with a map of the world.

Bunker Hill Community College in Boston engages in a variety of low-cost activities that further the college's global learning goal. Faculty and staff members from other countries and those who have traveled to other countries volunteer to host a seminar and dinner event for their faculty and staff colleagues. The seminar begins at 5:00, when the host presents a topic of his or her choice related to the country or its culture. The group then travels together to a local ethnic restaurant for a prearranged dinner featuring foods of that country. Since faculty and staff members pay their own dinner costs, the International Center need only cover the cost for the host. Each semester, the International Center selects topics for a Global

Issues Forum and invites faculty, staff, and students to participate in a panel presentation. Topics are usually cross-cultural in nature; for example, "Brides, Babies, and Burials" focused on marriage, childbirth, and death rituals in selected cultures. The International Center targets and works with selected classes to assure an audience and then markets the program collegewide. As is the case with most institutions, the Office of Student Activities at Bunker Hill has a budget that provides activities and entertainment for the college community. The International Center and a variety of international student groups have worked to internationalize the programs provided by Student Activities. Specifically, international student groups help to identify low-cost entertainment that reflects their cultures or speakers who would be of interest to the college community. The Global Learners Program matches each new international student with a volunteer from either the faculty or the staff to establish an informal intercultural exchange. The pairs engage in activities ranging from having lunch together to participating in family celebrations.

At **Daytona Beach Community College** (DBCC) in Florida, the Department of Modern Languages and the English Language Institute (ELI) have recognized that valuable educational opportunities exist for partnering the global student population in the increasingly culturally diverse community colleges of the 21st century. In 1996, these departments created FACE-TO-FACE: A Program to Integrate International Students, to incorporate creative academic and cultural activities into the curricula. The program's goals are to enrich and diversify the cultural, educational, and language experiences for the college's international students, defined as both American and non-native students.

Activities are tied to course work and are guided by teacher-organized interview sessions that allow students to concentrate on content in a formal setting. Instructors across varying disciplines arrange the sessions. For example, an instructor of a world religion course and an instructor of an English language communication course meet to determine the specific goals and assessment criteria. They may elect to concentrate on Islam, if the English language course is heavily populated with students from the Middle East. After the objectives are identified, the instructors compose a questionnaire to facilitate the students' interview session. Before the actual meeting, each instructor discusses the exchange with his or her students. In this manner, students receive defined expectations from the instructor. Instructors also encourage students to formulate their own personal expectations of the project. The session occurs during a scheduled class period or at another mutually agreed upon time and place. Following the interview session, students may be required to make an appropriate journal entry, present their reactions orally, or use the information gained in the interview as a source for a research project.

Once the interviews are conducted and the final reports are given, the task is completed. The students now have a firsthand experience upon which to formulate an opinion of the global community. The opportunity to dispel myths has been given, and a meaningful learning opportunity has occurred.

The benefits of participation in FACE-TO-FACE are multiple: After a formal exchange has taken place, DBCC's American and foreign students are more likely to participate in informal social and cultural activities scheduled on campus. There is greater student involvement in college-sponsored activities such as cultural festivals, the Global Friends International Student Organization, film festivals, language clubs, and intramural sports. In short, the formal educational experience acts as an icebreaker, providing an exciting learning event and an increased awareness of and appreciation for the international peer. A true sense of community begins to develop. And international students have gained an opportunity for practical application of their emerging English language skills.

Numerous collaborative activities have evolved at DBCC from the FACE-TO-FACE model. The variety and scope of these initiatives should provide our readers with a rich array of examples to spark the interest and involvement of faculty across disciplines:

- For the ELI/QUANTA International Friends' Project, American and international students adopt a partner for a semester of cultural exchange and enrichment.
- Modern Languages/Peer Connection pairs Spanish and French classes with English-as-a-second-language (ESL) classes for language practice.
- Conversation Partners allows interested American and international students to sign up for a conversation partner.
- ELI/Court Reporting Technology has ESL students acting as script readers of actual court documents, thus providing students of machine shorthand the opportunity to refine their skill in listening to international accents.
- In the ELI/Journalism program, international students are interviewed for feature articles in the student newspaper, *In Motion*.
- ELI/Technical Ethics focuses on ethical issues relative to employment.
- The ELI/Human Services project helps American students prepare for a career in counseling by teaching them about cultural differences in such matters as eye contact, physical space, greetings, and expression of empathy.
- ELI/World Religion offers a bridge from text to small group conversations exploring the rites and beliefs of other religions.

- ELI/Teaching Diverse Populations lets education majors observe a multiethnic class studying the English language.
- In ELI/Student Success, issues of cultural diversity are discussed. E-mail Friends links students at different campus sites, providing ESL students with an enjoyable way to use their developing written expressive skills.
- The American Welcome Program invites local citizens to welcome the college's international students by inviting a student to a family dinner or holiday celebration.
- ELI/College Composition Honors is a peer-tutoring partnership that provides additional one-on-one language support to ESL students.

Other partnerships under development will connect ELI students with those in courses such as Computers in Business and Comparative Government.

Johnson County Community College in Kansas invites students to enroll in the Intercultural Semester, an opportunity to "go global while staying local." The program offers an alternative to leaving the country and complements traditional classroom-based instruction. Students register for an integrated program that includes intercultural communication, study of the language and history of a particular culture, pairing with a language and culture partner, an intensive weekend intercultural retreat, and an internship or service learning component. Those who complete the program successfully are awarded a scholarship toward participation in a study-abroad experience.

Broome Community College in Binghamton, New York, has enrolled 100 to 150 international students from more than 30 countries each semester since the early 1970s. One way it has found to involve these students in the life of the community is through a guest lecture program called International Classroom, in which international students volunteer to speak about their countries in the local public schools (K-12). In return, community members, as well as college personnel, are encouraged to invite international students to their homes during holiday periods.

To assist international students in English language acquisition, the college matches them with students in foreign language classes who are studying their language. A program offered by the Learning Assistance Center called LingoNet also pairs up ESL and English-speaking students who have common interests and are willing to spend at least two hours a week together.

The active International Student Club frequently holds fundraisers on campus to help pay for club trips. The most popular fundraisers are the lunches and dinners they sponsor, where the international students prepare dishes from their native countries and set up tables to display pictures and artifacts that represent their cultures. At the dinners, they also provide entertainment for the 200 to 300 guests who attend. The division of Community Education organizes another series of International Dinners for the local community. Each meal focuses on a particular country; the college cafeteria prepares Indonesian food, for example, and a faculty member who has recently visited the country offers a short slide presentation. These International Dinners typically draw as many as 200 attendees who pay only for the cost of the meal.

In addition to flag displays used at international events, the college has used large-format world maps to project a global image. The history department found most useful a 6-by-8-foot map available at a local wallpaper store. The wallpaper was purchased for $60 and glued to a Masonite backing. The college maintenance staff put Plexiglas panels over the paper and built an oak frame for the map. These maps have now been placed in many classrooms, hallways, and even faculty offices. Students can frequently be seen pointing to and talking about places on the maps, often with one of the college's international students. An even larger 10-foot world map has been installed in the atrium of the science building, and a geology professor regularly tapes articles about world geological events on the Plexiglas and structures assignments around them. Finally, with funds remaining from an international education grant, world atlases were purchased for faculty offices.

North Hennepin Community College in Minnesota offers a program that enhances opportunities for international students to interact with their U.S. counterparts by sending them out as "ambassadors" to represent their home cultures in other classrooms on campus and for the K-12 schools and community organizations within the college's service area. Visiting a class or a meeting and talking about their homelands and their customs gives international students the opportunity to practice their English skills and make additional connections in the community, while at the same time personalizing the study of other peoples and cultures for their audiences.

The **Maricopa Community College District** in Arizona has established the International and Intercultural Education Innovation Grants, dedicating budgetary support for innovative global education programs at the 10 colleges in the Maricopa system. Applications are accepted three times a year and are reviewed according to accepted criteria. Faculty and administrators are eligible to propose projects that relate to the district's priorities for international and intercultural education, and selections are made by the districtwide steering committee for global education. Two types of projects funded by these grants suggest the potential for leveraging a modest amount of financial support into significant professional development opportunities. The Internationalizing the Curriculum Project offers a stipend to faculty who will engage in curriculum development activities to infuse international content into their courses. Three fellowship programs have also been established to support immersion experiences for faculty in Australia, China, and Mexico. Participants in the Australia program engage in a four-week reciprocal exchange, being hosted in Australia at the Riverina Institute of TAFE or at Charles Sturt University and then hosting an Australian colleague back at their home college. The China and Mexico programs provide a four-week summer immersion experience that may involve teaching, taking classes, guest lecturing, or other professional activities. The selection process for all innovation grants follows established criteria and seeks to distribute awards fairly among applicants from all 10 of the colleges in the district.

Among a variety of international and intercultural programs established at **Delta College** in Michigan is the opportunity for students to engage in a community service experience that focuses on raising global consciousness. Delta nursing students have supported family health workshops; residential construction students have volunteered for Habitat for Humanity and an Indian mission restoration project; and Honors Program members work with the Adopt-a-School program, to name just a few of the outreach activities. As more and more colleges embrace the value of service learning, clearly this is another way to incorporate global awareness into student life.

At **Crowder College** in Missouri, students in a World Religions class become e-mail pen pals with international students who attend a nearby university. Their instructor has established this partnership with the university so that students have the opportunity to learn personally and directly about the customs and beliefs of those who practice one of the religions they are studying. Later in the term, they are given the opportunity to visit the university and meet their "e-pal," typically an experience that solidifies awareness of diversity for students who live in a community that has very little.

Oakton Community College in Illinois recognized a number of years ago the multiple benefits of extending international experiences to college employees and developed a program of language instruction targeted to that population and offered during the workday. Under the project title Internationalizing Ourselves, the Department of Modern Languages conducted an assessment of interests and used the results to tailor a program of conversational language classes and language tables during the lunch hour. In this model, faculty, staff, and administrators come together weekly as a community of learners to learn a new language and its culture or to build on previous study. Instructors are compensated according to accepted practice for facilitators of a staff development activity. A primary goal of the project—to increase sensitivity to the cultural and linguistic diversity of the college, the communities we serve, and our country—was clearly accomplished, as participants commented frequently on how humbling it was to be inarticulate in another language, on their broadened cultural perspectives, and on a variety of social and community-building benefits.

To address the intercultural dimension, several years ago Oakton established the ACCORD Committee, Advocating a College Community of Respect for Diversity. The faculty, staff, and administrators serving on the committee meet regularly to address issues related to fostering sensitivity to the needs of a diverse community and to plan activities that heighten awareness and promote understanding. Representative activities include case study presentations at division meetings, AIDS Awareness Week, guest speakers, Oakton Celebrates Cultures Week, panel discussions, teach-ins, and more. Through the efforts of ACCORD, attention to diversity issues has been absorbed into a variety of existing campus programs and activities and has become a more prominent component of each of them.

Muskegon Community College in Michigan has instituted several programs that promote attention to diversity issues within the college community. The college offers to all faculty and staff, as well as members of the board of trustees, the opportunity to participate in the Institute for the Healing of Racism. This is a nine-week program in which participants discuss how they are personally influenced by racism, at the same time developing an understanding of how people of other cultures and backgrounds are affected by racism. The Diversity Committee invites community members to showcase artifacts from their heritage to inform the community. These displays have represented many cultures, including Mexican, Puerto Rican, Central American, Native American, and European Spanish. The Diversity Committee also sponsors programs that commemorate cultural icons and significant events. For example, on the Martin Luther King Jr. holiday, the committee invites public leaders to address the campus and community to share their perspectives on Dr. King and his contributions. The committee similarly sponsors a historical display by representatives of the Latino community for the Cinco de Mayo celebration.

Comments on Technology

Community colleges, like their sister institutions of higher education, are making increased use of technology to accomplish their internationalization goals, just as they do for other college operations, programs, and services. The Internet provides ready access to authentic materials for modern language instruction, to information from the world press, and to a wide variety of perspectives for essentially every discipline. Instructors are using such techniques as classroom-to-classroom linkages, through e-mail or real-time video links, so that students can engage in discussions, collaborative projects, and other global connections with fellow students around the world while never leaving their home campus. The impetus for virtual linkages is often a direct contact made by a faculty member with a colleague in another country. Thus, the faculty's own professional development experiences bring back an immediate and tangible benefit to students. Initiatives like these take the existing technologies in which our institutions have invested to another level of use and truly make it possible to operate on a global scale.

Conclusion

There is no single template that works for all colleges: The most successful programs derive from an assessment of the needs and interests of the college and its community. These programs capitalize on the in-house talents and experience to be found among college students, employees, and residents of the college's service area. Typically, they work within existing college resources and programs, such as professional development budgets, student activities programming, information technology, and curriculum development incentives, to direct established initiatives toward issues and activities that are international and intercultural. They frequently involve the contributions of international students or resident students of other cultures, and in so doing enrich the acculturation experiences of these students as members of the college and the community. And as we saw in the examples from Daytona Beach Community College, collaborative programs that link ESL students with their counterparts in a variety of disciplines can greatly benefit both groups. The possibilities are infinite! These are truly exciting times for community colleges in global education.

Bibliography

Davis, Todd, ed. 2000. *Open Doors 2000: Report on International Education Exchange*. New York: Institute of International Education.

CHAPTER 12

AACC INTERNATIONAL SERVICES

Audree M. Chase
Consultant, International Education Programs
Alexandria, Virginia

Internationalizing a community college campus involves many strategies direct-ed at addressing the needs of all interested stakeholders. Integral to this process is the commitment of the governing boards of two-year institutions to the importance of a global perspective so that it appears prominently in the college's mission statement. Administrators and faculty members must work together to accomplish goals set forth to advocate for advancing the global competency of all students who study at the institution. And there are many organizations out-side the college community that can be used to fulfill the mission of interna-tionalizing a campus.

This chapter will concentrate on the international activities and services provided by the American Association of Community Colleges (AACC) and will mention some of the organizations, external to the community college, that can assist in these important efforts.

AACC Mission

Since 1920, AACC has advocated for community colleges across the nation. The association acts on behalf of its more than 1,100 member colleges as a representa-tive to federal agencies; provides professional development activities for college leaders; and serves as a general repository of resources and data about community colleges. AACC monitors trends in areas such as legislative issues, workforce devel-opment, and minority services. It conducts research and interacts with other many other organizations as appropriate to fulfill the needs of its member colleges. The 24 affiliated councils of AACC work closely with the national organization to address special concerns and issues.

An important role of the association is to advocate for international edu-cation at community colleges. In unveiling its new mission statement, the AACC has made important strides in supporting the promotion of global aware-ness. Two components of the new statement include "supporting community colleges to prepare learners to be effective in a global society" and "empowering community colleges to grow as a global force for learning by disseminating information and promoting international partnerships between American community colleges and countries seeking collaborative opportunities" (2001).

To implement its new mission statement, AACC is concentrating on six strategic action areas. One of these areas specifically addresses the need to provide a global dimension to community college campuses. This strategic goal, "International and Intercultural Education," states that AACC will seek to have "community colleges prepare students for an increasingly global economy and society." The goal further states that the association will work "with appropriate councils and other organizations" and extend "the community college movement to other countries" (2001).

These new goals represent a strong move forward for AACC in the international arena. They represent a renewed commitment to the importance of producing a globally competent citizen—a new commitment built upon the work of the association in previous years.

Inside AACC

An important component of the international work within the AACC is the Commission on International/Intercultural Services. This commission advises the AACC board of directors and staff on new trends in international education and encourages new initiatives and services as a result of these trends. The commission was instrumental in rewriting the AACC Policy Statement on International Education, for example. Resources like these serve as proactive tools for college presidents and administrators to garner support for global efforts with their governing boards, on their campuses, and in their communities.

Ideally situated in Washington, D.C., representatives of AACC meet with more than 100 international delegates and visitors every year. These educational diplomats, from Albania to Zimbabwe, are keenly interested in the mission and purpose of the American community college system. The ideals of a community college are often not found in any segment of another country's educational system, and delegates are fascinated by short-term training, the emphasis on teaching and learning, the connectedness to the community, and the concept of lifelong learning. For all of the international delegations that find their way to AACC's open door, it is the association's role to educate them in the ways of the American community college. Often as a result of meeting with AACC staff members, international visitors wish to experience a community college firsthand, and the association works to arrange site visits accordingly. Recently, AACC arranged custom-designed study tours focusing on workforce development for Egyptian educators and on the governance of community colleges for educational diplomats from South Africa. When U.S. educators wish to examine models of higher education in other countries, AACC arranges professional study tours for them. Recent tours included the United Kingdom, Australia, and China.

AACC is assisted in its international work by one of its 24 affiliated councils: The American Council on International Intercultural Education (ACIIE), head-quartered at Oakton Community College in Illinois, is devoted exclusively to international education. AACC has traditionally worked closely with ACIIE to provide mutual support and promote international and intercultural education at community colleges nationwide. ACIIE has a membership of two-year institutions dedicated to enhancing international and intercultural programs on campus through the facilitation of programs, activities, and linkages. ACIIE has organized several important initiatives in support of its mission.

Among these notable efforts is the facilitation of conferences held in Warrenton, Virginia, funded by the Stanley Foundation, to address such topics as "Building the Global Community" and "Educating for the Global Community: A Framework for Community Colleges." The reports produced from these conferences have become standard references for community colleges that seek to get more involved in international education (ACIIE and Stanley 1995, 1997). ACIIE also surveys its members regularly to ascertain their level of involvement in international education and the nature of their projects to facilitate networking and the sharing of best practices.

Within AACC, the Office of International Services works to raise the visibility of international education at its member colleges. To accomplish this goal, it has adopted a three-pronged approach. The first is to work closely with federal agencies and domestic and international organizations to make them aware of the wealth of international programs at America's community colleges. The second is to assist member colleges in recruiting international students. The third is to assist member colleges in their development of international and intercultural programs by linking them with grant programs and organizations that will support their endeavors.

As part of its effort to collect and disseminate information, the Office of International Services conducted a national survey in 1995 on international programs at community colleges. This was the first research of its kind for the community college. Its purpose was to gauge the scope and breadth of international and intercultural programs at two-year institutions. Of the 1,200 AACC member colleges, more than 600 institutions responded. The findings of this survey proved that community colleges were involved with global education in dynamic and innovative ways. It also revealed that there was likely to be a growing interest in international programs within the next 5 to 10 years (Chase and Mahoney 1996). The association recently completed a follow-up study to this effort. Although the college response rate was far lower, it was determined that international programs have indeed grown significantly (Blair et al. 2001).

In cooperation with the National Foreign Language Center at Johns Hopkins University, AACC conducted another survey in 1996, to assess the status of foreign language education at community colleges. Results indicated that class enrollments for less commonly taught languages, such as Russian, were down, while enrollments in Spanish classes were skyrocketing. The survey also yielded intriguing information, such as the fact that a few community colleges are teaching such unusual languages as Swahili, Tagalog, and Welsh.

In addition to its own research on the community college, the association has resource publications available for its members such as George Vaughan's *The Community College Story* (2000), which has been translated into Spanish, French, Russian, and Chinese. This publication, a brief overview of the history, mission, and life of an American community college, is intended as a tool for international development projects and to recruit international students.

As part of an effort to enhance global education, AACC launched a Community College International Recruitment initiative in January 2002 to assist institutions with their international recruiting efforts and to elevate the profile of community colleges in global education and exchange. The initiative provides an opportunity for community colleges to attract students through a series of international recruitment fairs designed solely for two-year institutions and held in countries from which most international students originate. AACC introduced online international recruitment fairs as well, thus extending the fairs' reach worldwide without the travel costs. Information on the recruitment fairs is available on the Web at www.aacc.nche.edu/recruitmentfairs.

The AACC Office of International Services also provides information to member colleges wishing to apply for grants to develop their international programs. AACC researches and pursues other grant opportunities that are targeted to assist its member colleges in developing their international education programs. Some of these initiatives are mentioned below.

Work with Federal Agencies

AACC frequently works with the U.S. Department of Education, the U.S. Department of State, and the U.S. Agency for International Development (USAID) to promote the interests of community colleges and to make sure that they receive their fair share of grant monies. In the past, the association has also worked collaboratively with the U.S. Institute of Peace to organize a summer seminar for community college faculty addressing the subject of conflict resolution. Other federal organizations with which AACC works include the National Endowment for the Humanities and the National Science Foundation. In addition to fostering collaborative partnerships with these agencies, the association encourages them to provide grant opportunities for community colleges and to have representatives from member institutions serve on panels as proposal readers.

One recent federal initiative was a million-dollar grant from USAID titled Building International Workforce Development Partnerships. AACC implemented this project and worked in collaboration with the Association Liaison Office for University Cooperation in Development (ALO), which administered the initiative. ALO is an organization representing the interests of the six major higher educational associations with regard to their international development work with USAID. The purpose of this project was to encourage partnerships between American community colleges and institutions of higher education in developing nations for the purpose of workforce development and skills training. The AACC project aimed to address one of the overarching project goals, which was to "contribute to the preparation of a responsible citizenry and a proficient workforce engaged in a global marketplace" (ALO 2000).

The ALO project, which concluded in September 2001, involved at its peak nearly 20 community colleges. Projects ranged from exchanging culinary arts courses between a Hawaiian community college and the Ceylon School of Hospitality and Tourism in Sri Lanka to providing training in the handling of hazardous waste products for environmental technologists at the University of Tashkent in Uzbekistan. The partnerships also trained nurses in Russia, land surveyors in Guyana, information technology professionals in South Africa and Tanzania, and welders and electricians in Mexico. The highly successful ALO projects highlighted the training capacities of community colleges and provided foreign institutions with training necessary to assist their countries in moving toward a sustainable economy.

The Office of International Services works in tandem with the AACC Office of Government Relations, which monitors legislative actions as they pertain to international activities at community colleges. Examples of the legislation that AACC tracks include deeming (the practice of collecting extensive financial information from legal immigrants applying for federal student aid); funding for international education programs; and the Coordinated Interagency Program Regulating International Students (CIPRIS), now referred to as the Student and Exchange Visitor Information System (SEVIS). To further its goals, AACC is a member of the Alliance for International, Educational, and Cultural Exchange, which is an advocacy group that examines legislative actions as they relate to federally funded international education and exchange programs. In addition, representatives from AACC's Office of Government Relations and Office of International Services regularly attend working groups, consisting of representatives from other higher educational associations, to discuss and resolve issues of common interest.

Work with Other Organizations

AACC works collaboratively with other organizations to promote international education. Through its Washington office, AACC is able to reach out to the diplomatic community. Working collaboratively with the Association of Community College Trustees (ACCT), the association organized an embassy program during the annual National Legislative Seminar in Washington, D.C. For several years, AACC and ACCT offered teams of presidents and trustees the opportunity to meet with educational attachés from approximately 30 different countries. The purpose of these meetings was to share the community college mission and purpose, learn about concerns the attachés had for their students wishing to study at community colleges, and begin a dialogue between college and embassy officials to develop collaborative projects. The work with embassy officials is a great benefit to community colleges looking for partners abroad for a variety of projects.

AACC also works closely with the Community Colleges for International Development (CCID). CCID provides its members opportunities to promote economic development and build global relationships intended to strengthen educational programs. Chapter 6 contains further details on the work of CCID.

Joint projects among key entities in the community college world are critical to ensure widespread success. In the past, ACIIE, CCID, and AACC have collaborated to produce national videoconferences for community colleges interested in international education. Two of the most recent addressed the topic of international student recruitment, and a third, offered in November 2001, dealt with managing liability and risk in international programs.

AACC has worked with other domestic and international organizations in various capacities to advocate for international education at its member colleges. Some of these organizations include NAFSA:Association of International Educators, the Institute of International Education (IIE), and the College Consortium for International Studies (CCIS). AACC interacts with these organizations to ensure that they can provide cutting-edge information to its members as they seek to develop their international programs. Following is a brief description of these organizations.

NAFSA, located in Washington, D.C., "works to promote the exchange of students and scholars to and from the United States. . . . Members share a belief that international educational exchange advances learning and scholarship, builds respect among different peoples and encourages constructive leadership in a global community" (NAFSA 2001). Its primary responsibility is to advocate for legislative support of international programs. For example, NAFSA, working with the major higher education associations, was instrumental in securing support at the U.S. Departments of Education and State for the promotion of the first-ever International Education Week in November 2000. The organization also holds regional workshops for its members throughout the year to share best practices and encourage networking. NAFSA's Region VII, for example, established an Embassy Dialogue Committee, which encourages the exchange of information and concerns between educators and embassy officials in Washington, D.C.

The Institute of International Education (IIE), headquartered in New York City and with offices throughout the United States and the world, works to foster "the free flow of knowledge and ideas across national boundaries, in the conviction that no nation can prosper economically, culturally, or intellectually in isolation from the rest of the world" (IIE 2001). IIE conducts scholarly research on trends in international exchange and reports its findings in its annual publication *Open Doors*. The organization also provides education and training for professionals and students. It provides professional training for international visitors who are in the United States through the International Visitor Program, funded by the U.S. Department of State. In this regard, IIE contacts AACC representatives regularly to address international visitors or groups to explain the mission and purpose of the American community college.

The College Consortium for International Studies (CCIS) consists of two- and four-year institutions that share study-abroad programs geared primarily toward American undergraduate students. A more detailed description of the CCIS is provided in chapter 4.

Conclusion

Helping colleges establish and maintain their international programs, AACC, through its Office of International Services, serves as a resource and advocate for its members. It further seeks to promote the mission of the community college throughout the world. Because of its location, by virtue of its history, and reinforced by its bold new mission statement, the American Association of Community Colleges is committed to the importance of providing a global perspective at the community college level. The nature of the work at AACC means that a little of all of these elements is likely to occur on any given day. Thus

AACC is well suited to address the international educational needs of its members and all other interested stakeholders.

Bibliography

American Association of Community Colleges. 2001. "Mission Statement." Web site: www.aacc.nche.edu [Accessed: 16 October 2001].

American Council on International Intercultural Education and The Stanley Foundation. 1995. *Building the Global Community: The Next Step.* Conference report. Muscatine, Iowa: Stanley Foundation.

———. 1997. *Educating for the Global Community: A Framework for Community Colleges.* Conference report. Muscatine, Iowa: Stanley Foundation.

Association Liaison Office for University Cooperation in Development. 2000. Web site: www.aascu.org/alo [Accessed: 16 October 2001].

Blair, Donna, Lisa Phinney, and Kent A. Phillippe. 2001. *Research Brief: International Programs at Community Colleges.* Washington, D.C.: American Association of Community Colleges.

Chase, Audree M., and James R. Mahoney, eds. 1996. *Global Awareness in Community Colleges: A Report of a National Survey.* Washington, D.C.: Community College Press, American Association of Community Colleges.

Davis, Todd M., ed. 2000. *Open Doors 2000: Report on International Education Exchange.* New York: Institution of International Education.

Institute of International Education. 2001. "About IIE." Web site: www.iie.org [Accessed 17 October 2001].

NAFSA: Association of International Educators. 2001. "About NAFSA." Web site: www.nafsa.org [Accessed: 17 October 2001].

Vaughan, George B. 2000. *The Community College Story.* Washington, D.C.: Community College Press, American Association of Community Colleges.

Resources

Organizations and their Web sites mentioned in this chapter:

- Alliance for International, Educational, and Cultural Exchange: www.alliance-exchange.org
- American Association of Community Colleges: www.aacc.nche.edu
- American Council on International Intercultural Education: www.aciie.org

- Association of Community College Trustees: www.acct.org
- Association Liaison Office for University Cooperation in Development: www.aascu.org/alo
- College Consortium for International Studies: www.ccisabroad.org
- Community Colleges for International Development: www.kirkwood.cc.ia.us/ccid
- Institute of International Education: www.iie.org
- International Research and Exchanges Board (IREX): www.irex.org/programs/fsau/host_app.htm
- NAFSA: Association of International Educators: www.nafsa.org
- National Endowment for the Humanities: www.neh.gov
- National Foreign Language Center at The Johns Hopkins University: www.nflc.org
- National Science Foundation: www.nsf.gov
- U.S. Agency for International Development: www.info.usaid.gov
- U.S. Department of Education: www.ed.gov
- U.S. Department of State: www.state.gov
- U.S. Institute of Peace: www.usip.gov

FEDERAL FUNDING FOR COMMUNITY COLLEGE INTERNATIONAL EDUCATION PROGRAMS AND ACTIVITIES

Allen Cissell, U.S. Department of Education, Washington, D.C.
David Levin, U.S. Department of State, Washington, D.C.

Years ago, the *New Yorker* ran a cartoon that seemed to sum up how Washington, D.C., worked: Moses, coming down from the mountain, standing before the multitudes, the Ten Commandments cradled in his arms—and someone from the crowd yelling, "Sure, but what about funding?"

This chapter is about funding for international programs and activities. It lists many of the U.S. government programs that provide financial support needed to implement the "commandments" contained in the previous chapters. It is not intended to be a comprehensive list but only a guide to major funding sources. Many federal departments and agencies have funding for international activities, although most of the programs are not relevant to community colleges. The sources of funding listed in this chapter have proved their value over the years and are sponsored by the U.S. government agencies that are best known both for international education efforts and for exhibiting a keen interest in serving community colleges. Although government funding opportunities may rise and fall with national priorities, the programs and activities we have listed are the most likely to be continual sources of support for international education activities both at home and abroad.

In addition to the programs listed in this chapter, the Interagency Working Group on U.S. Government–Sponsored International Exchange and Training (IAWG), a 27-agency working group chaired and staffed by the U.S. Department of State, compiles an annual report listing the wide range of federally sponsored programs and activities in international education, international exchange, and training. The report is available online at the following Web site: www.iawg.gov/info/reports/public_indexreports.html.

Beyond providing information about funding opportunities, this chapter offers comments and suggestions on grantsmanship—how to write and submit successful applications and proposals. Though not all-encompassing, these comments and suggestions reflect our perspectives based on having been program directors, evaluating hundreds of individual and institutional proposals submitted by applicants ranging from small rural colleges to the most prestigious universities in the United States.

We encourage community colleges and their students, faculty, and staff to submit proposals to these various programs. Forty-four percent of undergraduate students in the United States are enrolled in community colleges. It is critical that these students learn about other peoples, including their cultures and languages, and about the globalization of important issues affecting all of us, such as health, business and trade, environment, education, and politics. It is the responsibility of the higher education community to assist its clientele in developing a global perspective based on international awareness and understanding. The programs listed below are designed to assist in that effort. Program managers are seeking additional applicants. This is true for institutional grant programs open to higher education institutions as well as for the different grant opportunities open to individuals on college and university campuses. Community colleges and their students, faculty, and staff are particularly encouraged to apply in greater numbers. With a number of these programs, the ratio of applicants to grants awarded is every bit as good for community colleges as it is for higher education as a whole.

U.S. Department of Education

Within the U.S. Department of Education, there are seven programs to explore as possible funding sources for international education programs. Four of these are found within the International Education and Graduate Programs Service (IEGPS) and three are in the Fund for the Improvement of Postsecondary Education (FIPSE). Each of these programs is detailed below.

International Education and Graduate Programs Service

The Fulbright Group Projects Abroad Program is one of two Fulbright programs administered by the Department of Education open to community colleges. Four types of projects can be funded under this program: short-term seminars; curriculum development teams; group research or study projects; and advanced overseas intensive language projects. However, most of the awards are made in the category of short-term seminars. These seminars are four to six weeks long and focus on a specific topic. The applicant institution designs a project (e.g., the study of mythology in Mexico) and then recruits participants. In this example, participants were Spanish language teachers recruited from several colleges and from secondary schools in the local area. Most of the costs associated with these projects (airfares, hotel, etc.) are paid from grant funds, and an average grant is approximately

$60,000. Forty grants are projected for the coming year. For more information, visit the IEGPS Web site at www.ed.gov/offices/OPE/HEP/iegps.

The Fulbright Seminars Abroad Program is the second of the Fulbright programs administered by the Department of Education open to community college faculty. This program requires an application directly from individual K-12 educators and college faculty members. Department of Education staff and binational Fulbright Commissions abroad work together to design the seminar content, format, and travel agenda. Recent examples of seminar sites include Morocco and Tunisia, South Africa, Turkey and Bulgaria, India and Nepal, Mexico, Argentina, Israel and Jordan, China and Malaysia, and Singapore. The Department of Education expects to fund about 10 such seminars annually, with 16 to 18 slots for each seminar. In 2002, one seminar will be held specifically for community college faculty only. Most seminar costs are paid by the grants, although some predeparture costs may be assessed. Applicants must be from the social sciences or the humanities, have at least three years of full-time teaching experience, and be employed full time at their college. For additional information, visit the IEGPS Web site: www.ed.gov/offices/OPE/HEP/iegps.

The Business and International Education Program, authorized by Title VI-B of the Higher Education Act, promotes "education and training that will contribute to the ability of U.S. businesses to prosper in an international economy." The program makes two-year awards (the average grant is around $75,000) to colleges and universities to carry out this goal through such activities as internationalization of the business curricula, establishment of export education programs, support for student and faculty fellowships, development of new programs for midcareer or part-time students, etc. A 50 percent cost-share is required, which can be monetary or in kind, and each applicant must submit evidence of an agreement with a business enterprise to increase the likelihood of the project's success (e.g., one might have an agreement to place faculty in an internship with a company that exports a product or service). For more information, visit the IEGPS Web site: www.ed.gov.offices/OPE/HEP/iegps.

The Undergraduate International Studies and Foreign Language Program, authorized under Title VI-A of the Higher Education Act, encourages colleges, individually or in combination, to carry out activities that "strengthen and improve" undergraduate instruction in international studies and foreign languages. An institutional match of 50 percent of the total cost of the program is required. This can be monetary or in kind and can come from sources other than the institution itself (e.g., state or private contributions). Program activities must focus on both international studies and foreign language activities to be eligible. Activities might include the development of study-abroad programs, internships for faculty or students, the development of an international studies program or a top-ical program (e.g., international health programs), the development of curricula for preprofessional studies, etc. Grants are usually for a two-year period but may be for three years for consortia applications. Grants average $70,000 per year. For more information, visit the IEGPS Web site: www.ed.gov/offices/OPE/HEP/iegps.

Fund for the Improvement of Postsecondary Education

The Fund for the Improvement of Postsecondary Education (FIPSE) administers three international programs, representing special relationships between the Department of Education and foreign government agencies. These are (1) the Program for North American Mobility in Higher Education (U.S., Canada, and Mexico); (2) the European Commission–United States Joint Consortia for Cooperation in Higher Education and Vocational Education (the EC-U.S. Program); and (3) the U.S.-Brazil Higher Education Consortia Program (U.S.-Brazil Program). All are consortia programs, requiring cooperation with multiple institutions here and abroad (FIPSE staff will help arrange these partnership agreements) and are generally funded by both U.S. and foreign governments for three or four years' duration. Funding has supported significant efforts in student exchange, development of apprenticeships, faculty exchange, articulation agreements, and other areas. For additional information on the North American Mobility program, contact Sylvia.Crowder@ed.gov. For the EC-U.S. Program, contact Frank.Frankfort@ed.gov. For the U.S.-Brazil Program, contact Mike.Nugent@ed.gov.

U.S. Department of State
Bureau of Educational and Cultural Affairs

The U.S. Department of State, through its Bureau of Educational and Cultural Affairs (ECA), sponsors and administers a wide range of academic, professional, and cultural programs and activities that foster mutual understanding between U.S. citizens and people from other countries worldwide. The bureau's academic offerings include programs for students, teachers, and scholars, including the flagship Fulbright exchanges, university-to-university linkages, English-as-a-second-language efforts, and foreign student advising services abroad. Professional and cultural exchanges include grassroots, thematic citizen exchange programs involving the private sectors in the United States and overseas, professional programming for international visitors from abroad, youth exchange programs, and programs in culture and the arts. For additional information about the entire range of bureau-funded programs and activities, refer to the bureau's Web site at www.exchanges.state.gov.

The following 18 ECA programs and activities are relevant to community colleges and their students, faculty, or staff:

The Citizen Exchanges Program provides institutional grants to nonprofit American institutions, including community organizations, professional associations, and colleges and universities, to support two-way exchange partnerships with like institutions and organizations abroad. Programs operate worldwide. Projects are thematically based and include such areas as conflict resolution, civic education, media development, rule of law, environmental protection, trade unionism, judicial reform, local government, civil and human rights protection, nongovernmental organization (NGO) development, citizen networking, legislative reform, intellectual property rights, public administration, small business development, management training, and visual and performing arts. Activities often include U.S.-based seminars and site visits, and in-country workshops. Individualized internships and home stays with American families are also part of this program. Several requests for grant proposals (RFGPs) are issued annually addressing specific themes and relating to specific world areas. For additional information, refer to the program's Web site: exchanges.state.gov/education/citizens.

The Community Connections Program awards grants to U.S. community-based nongovernmental organizations, as well as to colleges and universities, to provide home stay–based, three- to five-week practical training/internship opportunities for professionals from the New Independent States of the former Soviet Union. Participants may include entrepreneurs, local government officials, legal professionals, NGO leaders, and other professionals from Armenia, Azerbaijan, Belarus, Georgia, Kazakhstan, Moldova, Russia, and the Ukraine. Institutional grants are for $100,000 and up, depending upon the number of groups hosted and the location. For additional information, contact the Community Connections program staff by telephone or refer to the program's Web site: exchanges.state.gov/education/citizens/comcon.

The Congress-Bundestag Exchange Program provides grants to enable U.S. and German high school students and young professionals to spend a year abroad while living with host families. The purpose is to promote better understanding between Germany and the United States. High school students attend a high school abroad for one academic year. "Young Professionals," aged 18 to 24, combine study at a community college, technical college, or professional school with a company-based internship. The program annually funds 800 Americans and 800 Germans, with most participant costs covered by the grant. Community college students often participate in this program during or after having completed their associate degree studies. For additional information about grants for Americans or about hosting German participants, refer to the

CDS International Web site at www.cdsintl.org, or contact CDS International by e-mail at cbyx@cdsintl.org.

The Cooperative Grants Program (COOP) awards seed grants to institutions of higher education and to nonprofit organizations for campus- or community-based projects that involve U.S. international students and U.S. study-abroad students on American campuses and in American communities. The program is particularly interested in receiving proposals from minority-serving institutions, community organizations, and community colleges. Proposals should meet one or more of the program's three purposes: (1) to encourage foreign students and scholars at U.S. colleges and universities to become involved in and knowledgeable about U.S. culture and society; (2) to enhance the experiences of U.S. study-abroad students prior to their departure or after their return; and (3) to stimulate and strengthen interaction among international students and their U.S. peers, faculty, and communities. Grants are made in three categories: (1) incentive grants of between $2,001 and $10,000, (2) minigrants of up to $2,000, and (3) International Education Week Grants of up to $2,000. All funds must be spent in the United States. In the case of the third grant category, proposals, in addition to meeting one or more of the program's three purposes, should work to raise campus and community awareness of international education and global issues and should plan to have the funded activities take place during International Education Week. For further information about COOP, an application packet, and a Model Programs list that describes 100 recently funded projects, refer to the COOP Web site: www.nafsa.org/content/professionalandeducationalresources/grantsandscholarship/grantsandscholarships.html.

The Educational Partnerships Program (previously known as the College and University Affiliations Program) supports educational partnerships between U.S. colleges and universities and foreign postsecondary institutions through faculty and staff exchanges on themes of mutual interest, based on U.S. and foreign institutional partners' assessed capabilities and needs. Eligible disciplines include the social sciences, humanities, law, business, journalism, communications, educational administration, and public health policy and administration. The program operates in all world regions except for the New Independent States (NIS) of the former Soviet Union (linkage grants with institutions in the NIS are supported under other Department of State programs detailed elsewhere in this chapter). Eligibility of countries within each world region generally rotates on a three-year period. Grants typically range from $100,000 to $150,000 for a three-year period. For additional information, contact the Humphrey Fellowships and Institutional Linkages Branch by telephone or refer to the program's Web site: exchanges.state.gov/education/CUAP.

The **English Language Fellows Program** awards grants to experienced teacher trainers and recent M.A. graduates to work abroad in host country ministries of education, universities, and binational centers. The program operates worldwide. Awards are for 11 months, with fellows teaching English as a foreign language (EFL) and English for special purposes (ESP), and carrying out special projects in teacher training, methodology, curriculum development, and needs analysis. Grants range from $35,000 to $55,000, depending on the level of assignment. For further information, contact the School for International Training (SIT) by telephone or refer to the SIT Web site at sit.edu.

The **English Language Specialists Program** awards grants to American academics in the fields of teaching English as a foreign language (TEFL), teaching English as a second language (TESL), and applied linguistics for short-term assignments worldwide. Participants conduct conferences and workshops and consult in areas of curriculum design, teacher training, and textbook development. Grants are for two weeks to six weeks and include travel, per diem, honorarium, and other incidental costs. Applicants should have an M.A. or Ph.D. in TEFL/TESL or applied linguistics, teacher training experience, and overseas experience. For more information, see the Web site: http://exchanges.state.gov/education/engteaching/specialists.htm/.

The **Freedom Support Act Undergraduate Program** provides scholarships to undergraduate students from the New Independent States of the former Soviet Union to pursue an academic year of nondegree study in the United States. Fields include agriculture, American studies, business, computer science, economics, environmental management, journalism/mass communication, political science, and sociology. Students live with host families, and their academic studies are enhanced through community service activities, a practical internship and orientation, and end-of-year workshops. Approximately 300 awards are available annually, and grants cover most costs. Grantee recruitment, selection, and placement are administered by the International Research and Exchanges Board (IREX). Community colleges interested in hosting students under this program should refer to the IREX Web site: http://www.irex.org/programs/fsau/host_app.htm/.

The **Fulbright Occasional Lecturer Program** provides support for foreign Fulbright scholars and professionals already on assignment in the United States to visit other campuses for a two- to five-day period. The purpose of these visits is for the scholars to participate in conferences and symposia, to offer teaching and training for students and faculty, to participate in community activities, and to engage in other activities that promote cross-cultural, international understanding. The program covers grantee travel while the host institution arranges accommodations and covers local costs. Visits may be arranged by the scholars themselves or through invitations from colleges and universities. For additional information, including an online directory of the Visiting Fulbright Scholars in the United States for the current academic year, visit the Council for International Exchange of Scholars (CIES) Web site at: www.cies.org/cies/usinst.html.

The Fulbright Scholar-in-Residence Program provides grants to enable U.S. colleges and universities to host visiting lecturers from abroad for a semester or academic year. Preference is given to institutions that are traditionally less involved in international exchange programs, including hosting visiting scholars, or that are serving minority audiences. Priority institutions include historically black colleges and universities, Hispanic-serving institutions, tribal colleges, small liberal arts colleges, and community colleges. The program operates worldwide. Subject fields include the social sciences, humanities, and a range of other fields. Grants range up to $35,000, depending upon the grant length and location. Host institutions are expected to provide some type of cost-share, in funds or in kind. Applications from consortia are welcomed. Institutional applications may designate a specific scholar by name, or request that one be recruited by U.S. embassies or binational Fulbright Commissions abroad. For additional information and application materials, refer to the Council for International Exchange of Scholars (CIES) Web site: www.cies.org/cies/usinst.html.

The Fulbright Senior Specialist Program awards grants to U.S. faculty and professionals to collaborate with academic institutions abroad in a wide variety of short-term projects and activities. The program operates worldwide. Specific opportunities are determined based on institutional requests from abroad, and U.S. citizens are matched against requests. Types of activities include conducting needs assessments and surveys, taking part in specialized academic programs and conferences, consulting on faculty development efforts, lecturing, conducting teacher training activities, and developing and assessing academic curricula or educational materials. The program operates in a wide range of subject fields and disciplines. Grants cover travel, per diem, and a daily honorarium. Applicants need to hold a Ph.D. or equivalent professional or terminal degree. Professionals and artists outside academe need to have recognized professional standing and substantial professional accomplishments. For additional information, including procedures for being added to the roster of specialists available to participate in the program, visit the Council for International Exchange of Scholars Web site: www.cies.org/cies/specialists.

The Fulbright Teacher and Administrator Exchange Program provides opportunities for U.S. teachers, administrators, and other school or college faculty to participate in direct exchanges of positions and in reciprocal exchanges with colleagues from other countries. Annually, 250 U.S. teachers and administrators participate in the program. Program length ranges from six weeks to an academic semester to an academic year in length. Opportunities exist for U.S. community college faculty and administrators in the Western Hemisphere, Western and Eastern Europe, the Baltics, East Asia, and Sub-Saharan Africa. Grant awards vary based on the length and type of program and the partner country involved. Applicants must have a current full-time teaching or administrative assignment and, generally, at least three years of teaching or administrative experience. For further information and application materials, refer to the following Web site: www.grad.usda/international.

The Fulbright U.S. Scholar Program awards grants to U.S. college faculty and professionals to lecture or conduct research abroad. Approximately 800 grants are offered annually, from two months to an academic year in length, in 140 countries worldwide. Nearly 40 disciplines are included, with large numbers of grants in the social sciences and the humanities. Grants range from $10,000 to $60,000 and up, based on grant duration and country of assignment. Applicants should hold a master's degree or Ph.D. or equivalent professional or terminal degree, depending on the specific assignment being sought. For the many lecturing awards offered, applicants should have college or university teaching experience at the level required in the field of the particular assignment, or have equivalent nonacademic professional experience. For further information, including application materials, refer to the CIES Web site at www.cies.org.

The Benjamin A. Gilman International Scholarship Program awards grants of up to $5,000 to U.S. undergraduate students to support study-abroad experiences worldwide. Applicants must be receiving need-based student assistance from the federal government under Title IV of the Higher Education Act. Study-abroad programs may be for a few weeks to up to an academic year in length and must be approved for credit by the student's home institution. For further information and application materials, refer to the following Web site: www.iie.org/gilman.

The International Visitors Program brings nearly 5,000 international visitors to the United States annually in the fields of labor, government, education, business, media, science, and the arts. Visitors, identified as future leaders in their home countries, are nominated for program participation by U.S. embassies abroad. Typically, visitors spend from one to three weeks in the United States, as individuals or as part of group projects, conferring with professional colleagues and experiencing America and Americans firsthand. Community colleges interested in hosting such visitors should contact the Council for International Visitors (CIV) nearest them to discuss possibilities. A list of the 100 visitors' councils in the United States, all part of the National Council for International Visitors (NCIV), can be found at www.nciv.org.

The National Clearinghouse on Disability and Exchange (NCDE), with multiyear funding from the Department of State, seeks to increase the number of people with disabilities participating in international exchange programs. Managed by Mobility International USA, the NCDE works (1) to provide information about the wide range of international exchange opportunities available to people with disabilities and (2) to provide exchange organizations and colleges and universities with technical assistance about how to increase the number of disabled people participating in their exchange programs. Clearinghouse activities include information and referral through an extensive database and Web site, publications and videos, media campaigns, and other outreach efforts, as well as training offered through NCDE participation in conference, seminars, and workshops. For further information about the Clearinghouse's programs, products, and services, refer to the following Web site: www.miusa, or contact the Clearinghouse by e-mail at ncde@miusa.org.

The New Independent States College and University Partnership Program funds educational partnerships between U.S. colleges and universities and similar higher education institutions in the New Independent States (NIS) of the former Soviet Union, including Georgia, Kazakhstan, Moldova, Russia, Ukraine, and Uzbekistan. For fiscal year 2002, a special program will be conducted specifically for community colleges—the New Independent States Community College Partnership Program—to enable community colleges to collaborate with like institutions in these same NIS countries. Subject fields include communication/journalism, law, business/accounting/trade, education/education administration/continuing education, public policy and administration, and social, political, and economic sciences. Grants range up to $300,000 for a three-year period, depending on the specific program component. For further information about both programs, including application guidelines and deadlines, call the Humphrey Fellowships and Institutional Linkages Branch or refer to the program's Web site: exchanges.state.gov/education/NISCUPP.

Overseas Education Information Centers offer advice and guidance to foreign students considering study in the United States. More than 400 offices abroad, located in U.S. embassies and consulates, Fulbright Commission offices, and U.S. nonprofit organizations and other sites, offer a wide range of information for foreign students and scholars regarding educational opportunities in the United States. The information centers also provide individual and group advising on such topics as standardized testing, financial aid, application procedures, and living in the United States. Community colleges interested in providing information about their institutions to these advising centers as a recruitment tool can find a list of the centers, including mailing and email addresses, at the following Web site: exchanges.state.gov/education/educationusa.

U. S. Department of Commerce

In recent years, the Department of Commerce has been active in helping U.S. institutions of higher education "export" their services and recruit foreign students to their campuses. Through more than 100 Export Assistance Centers located around the United States and through the Department of Commerce's commercial service officers located at U.S. embassies abroad, the department provides, at no cost, reports on opportunities for activities with foreign institutions and companies. For a fee, centers will help identify international education fairs, facilitate college presences and exhibits at these fairs, identify potential educational partners, and set up overseas appointments with educators in specific countries. To contact any of the Export Assistance Centers in the United States, visit the following Web site: www.usatrade.gov.

U. S. Department of Defense
National Security Education Program

The Department of Defense's National Security Education Program awards David L. Boren scholarships to U.S. undergraduates, including community college students, to study abroad in geographic areas critical to U.S. national security. These include all world areas except Australia, New Zealand, Canada, and Western Europe. U.S. citizenship is required. Approximately 175 grants are awarded annually, ranging from $4,000 to $10,000 per academic term, covering such expenses as travel, tuition, books, or maintenance. Grants are for a minimum of one academic term, although six-week summer programs are possible. Students may study a broad range of subjects, and their time abroad must include studying the language of the host country. All grant recipients must subsequently fulfill a service requirement, working for a federal agency or office with national security responsibilities or in higher education in a field of study related to their grant award, for a period of time equal to the length of the award. For further information, including a listing of eligible countries, fields, and languages that the program defines as critical to national security, visit the following Web site: www.iie.org/nsep.

The **National Security Education Program** also awards institutional grants to U.S. two-year and four-year colleges and universities to build or enhance programs of study in foreign world areas and other fields and in languages critical to U.S. national security. Grants to support program and institutional infrastructure, program sustainability, and dissemination range up to $450,000 over a four-year time period. Institutional grants are also available to support materials and resource development in these same fields and subjects at two different levels—a maximum of $300,000 over a two-year period or a "minigrant" ranging from $25,000 to $75,000. For further information, including a listing of eligible countries, fields, and languages critical to national security, refer to the National Security Education Program Web site: www.ndu.edu/nsep.

U.S. Agency for International Development

The U.S. Agency for International Development (USAID), through its Center for Human Capacity Development, sponsors an institutional grant program supporting Workforce Development Partnerships between U.S. community colleges and similar institutions located in developing countries abroad. The program is administered by the Association Liaison Office for University Cooperation in Development. These competitive grants are to model community education systems to improve skills of the workforce for productive sectors in societies. Grants are for $100,000 over a two-year or three-year time period and require matching funds of at least $25,000. Past experience has demonstrated that partnerships of this nature have leveraged $2 for every $1 of USAID investment. Grant opportunities are announced annually, in February or March. Application materials and sample partnership profiles can be found on the following Web site: www.aascu.org.

Recommendations for Successful Grant Writing

Our recommendations for successful proposal writing and submission, whether for individual grants or for institutional awards, are based on what we have seen and reviewed over many years. While some comments and suggestions may seem basic, it is often the basic rules that are not followed, with predictably negative results.

First, and critical, be informed about the funding agency, the purposes of the program to which you are applying, and your eligibility. What are the objectives of the program? Why is the program important to you or to your institution? Do your interests and needs mesh with the program funder's stated philosophy and mission?

Second, make contact with the program officer administering the program, by e-mail, by telephone, or in person. Share your ideas regarding what you would like funded. Clarify program objectives and program requirements. It is recommended that you ask for copies of previously successful proposals, or abstracts (if available), to get a sense of the structure and substance of a proposal. If such information is not available, ask to talk with grantees that have competed successfully in the program and seek their advice and counsel.

Third, consider submitting a proposal in partnership with other colleges and universities. If your institution is small, is less able to meet the matching requirements of some grants, has insufficient experience in grant writing, or if you see programmatic advantages through collaboration, a consortial application may be especially advantageous. Generally, consortia proposals are well received in Washington, giving "more bang for the buck"—and some programs even allow for a longer funding period for such joint proposals.

Fourth, read the RFGP (request for grant proposals)/application instructions thoroughly before writing the proposal, and follow them exactly as you go through the process. Review and fully understand the criteria against which proposals will be evaluated. These criteria are almost always spelled out for you. Remember that reviewers are instructed to assess proposals against each and every criterion. For example, one of us recently read proposals in which a criterion was a minimal in-kind match by the partner institution. The first proposal read had a zero match—and was immediately disqualified. Other proposals were written for nonapproved areas of activity. It is essential that your application address all stated review criteria.

Fifth, include an evaluation component in your proposal. Because of the passage of the Government Performance and Results Act (GPRA) a few years ago, proposals now require greater attention to program outcomes. Your proposal should include an evaluation plan. What is measurable? Whom will it affect? What are the proposed outcomes? Who will measure or evaluate these outcomes and what are their qualifications? How will the evaluations be reported to the funding agency? Your application should address every review criterion, but the evaluation component is a very important part of an application.

Sixth, make your budget submission as clear and specific as possible. This is an area where many proposals lose points, as reviewers note, for example, that costs for selected items have not been included, other costs are unreasonable, or budget items are not spelled out or justified. Does your budget submission cover all costs? Additionally, if a "match" is required by the RFGP, and the proposal does not clearly identify it, the application will suffer. Have you shown all your in-kind contributions? If an institution can show that it is making a cash or non-cash commitment to the effort, even when not required by the program, it is likely to be considered a stronger proposal.

Seventh, ask someone not associated with the writing of the proposal to read it thoroughly and carefully for clarity and definition and for grammar, typos, jargon, acronyms, and consistency. Then run the proposal through your computer's spell check and grammar check. While proposals with missing sections, misassembled pages, or grammatical errors are not disqualified, these kinds of problems negatively affect readers' general impressions of the proposal.

Eighth, meet all the program's technical requirements. Have you completed and included all the required reporting forms? Have you included resumes, if necessary? Did you include required institutional financial reports? Does your application include supporting recommendations or letters of reference? Have you obtained the necessary institutional signoffs and signatures? Does your proposal fall within the maximum length allowed?

Ninth, if at first you do not succeed, try again. If you are not funded, ask for copies of the reviewers' comments, if they are not automatically sent by the funding agency. Generally, these comments will spell out the weaknesses of the proposal and allow you to revise your proposal for the next application cycle, should you wish to apply again. Many unsuccessful proposals are improved upon and funded the second time around.

Tenth, in a more general context, we encourage grant seekers to volunteer to serve as program reviewers (you will be paid, if selected). Overall, community colleges are not well represented among the reader pool (and not just for international education programs, but for many other programs as well). We maintain that there is no better way to learn about a program, or the review process, or how to write a successful proposal, than to serve as a reviewer. To initiate this process, send a resume to the program officer and indicate that you would like to serve in this capacity.

We hope this overview of the major federal international education programs of interest to community colleges, and our comments and suggestions, will assist community colleges to successfully compete for funds to support their international education activities.

INDEX

Austin Community College (Texas), 81–90
Australia, and faculty immersion experiences, 132
Austria, study-abroad center in, 93

B

Barents Euro-Arctic Region (BEAR), 78–79
Barnett, Lynn, 60
Beauchamp, Fay, xvi
Bennett, Milton J., 38
Berry, Howard, 60–61
board of trustees, of community college, 15, 97
branch campuses abroad, 92, 95
brochures, for international recruitment, 22–23
Brookdale Community College (New Jersey), 62
Broome Community College (New York), 63, 72, 79, 130–31
Broward Community College (Florida), 92–98
budget, as element in grant proposal, 157. See also funding
Bunker Hill Community College (Massachusetts), 127–28
business education, 147; as element of partnerships abroad, 99–106
businesses, local, and international trade, 100–104

C

campus support, for international students. See support services
Canada, and student exchange programs, 87–90
Caribbean Conference, CCID and, 75
Caribbean region, and partnerships abroad, 74–77
Centers for Academic Programs Abroad (CAPA), 50
Centro Integral Comunitario, 65
Chandler, Alice, 34
Chase, Audree, xvi

China, and faculty immersion experiences, 132
Chisholm, Linda, 60–61
Cissell, Allen, xvi
cocurricular project, service learning as, 66–67
College Board, 28–29
College Consortium for International Studies (CCIS), xiii, xiv, 11, 50–51, 61–63, 93, 140–41
College of Staten Island/CUNY (New York), 62
Colorado Mountain College, 67
Columbia University, 115
communication options, for international students, 41
community collaboration, and international education, 10
Community College Humanities Association (CCHA), 122
Community College of Philadelphia, 111–24
community colleges, 7–8, 11, 131–32, 137–38; and economic benefits of international students, 10–11, 13; and international affiliates, 94; and partnerships abroad, 99–100; and partnerships with universities, 139; and service-learning programs, 61–68; and small-scale international projects, 125–34; and study-abroad programs, 45–47, 56
Community Colleges for International Development (CCID), xiii, xv, 7, 71–73, 88, 140; work in Caribbean region, 74–77; work in India, 73–74; work in Latin America, 77–78; work in Russia/Norway, 78–79
community college students. See international students; service-learning programs; student exchange programs; study-abroad programs; transfer options
community resources, for international students, 42
community service experiences, for students, 132

community task force, for international recruitment, 18

COMPRO (Computerized Processes in Enterprises Involving Emerging High-Technology Occupations) student exchange program, 82–87

conference participation, faculty and, 122–23

consortial approach, 148, 157; for student exchange programs, 87–90; for study-abroad programs, 50–51, 82–87

consular interview, for international students, 23

Contract for Instructional Services, as part of affiliate program, 95

Corporation for National Service, 65

Costa Rica, study-abroad center in, 93

Council on International Educational Exchange (CIEE), 50

Council for International Visitors, 153

counseling services, for international students, 40–41. *See also* advisers, for international students

course credit, for study-abroad programs, 52

course development, 114–15. *See also* curriculum development

course infusion, 114

course integration, in ESL programs, 34–35

course modules, creating, 114

Crowder College (Missouri), 132

cultural artifacts, displayed on campus, 133

cultural component, in student exchange program, 85, 87

cultural diversity, 8–9, 11, 37–39, 133

cultural immersion, 86

cultural interaction: in student exchange programs, 89; in study-abroad programs, 54

cultural issues, for international affiliate programs, 97–98

culture, defined, 38

culture curriculum, for international students, 37–39

curriculum, xii, 7; links to study abroad, 52–53; for student exchange programs, 81, 83, 85, 89–90

curriculum development, xiii, 113–15, 131–32; area-studies approach, 111–24; as part of partnerships abroad, 102, 106–8

D

Davenport Chamber of Commerce, 102

Daytona Beach Community College (Florida), 77, 79, 128–30

degree requirements, and study-abroad programs, 53

Dellow, Donald A., xiv

Delta College (Michigan), 132

development activities, as focus of partnerships abroad, 73–80

Dewey, John, 59, 119

direct enrollment programs, for study abroad, 49

director of international education, and affiliate programs, 94

disabled people, exchange programs for, 154

displays, of cultural artifacts, 133

dissemination, of area-studies research, 121–23

distance learning, and international recruitment, 19–20

diversity issues, 8–9, 11, 37–39, 133

Dominican Republic, service-learning program in, 63

Dresden Chamber of Industry and Commerce (Germany), 83

Drohobych State Pedagogical University (Ukraine), 106–8

Dudderar, Jody, xiv

E

Eastern Europe; and faculty exchange program, 80; and partnerships abroad, 72

Eastern Iowa Community College District (EICCD), 73–75; Community College Partnership with

technical assistance program, Universidad Don Bosco (El Salvador), 77–78

technical development, and international education, 10

technical education, in COMPRO program, 82–87

technology, classroom, 107–8, 133–34

Technology for Industry through Mobility in Educational Sectors (TIMES) student exchange program, 87–90

Temple University, 113

terrorism and terrorist attacks, 2

trade missions, 104

transfer options, 94–96

transfer policy, for affiliate programs, 94–95

transfer programs, for international students, 18

tuition, for international students, 25–27

U

Ukraine, and partnership programs, 106–8, 154

United Arab Emirates, Centre for American Education (Dubai), 93–94, 96

Universidad del Valle de México, 95

Universidad de Tecnológico de Tula-Tepeji (Mexico), 88

Universidad Don Bosco, technical assistance program, 77–78

Universidad Nacional Autónoma de México, 95

Universidad Tecnológica de Coahuila (Saltillo, Mexico), 88

University College of the Cariboo (British Columbia, Canada), 88

University of Chicago, 115, 119

University of Hawaii, 114–15

University of Maryland, University College, 92

University of Pennsylvania, 115

University of Southern California, 56

U.S. Agency for International Development, 101, 138; Association Liaison Office, 108; Building International Workforce Development Partnerships, 139; Center for Human Capacity Development, 156; Workforce Development Partnerships, 156

U.S. Department of Commerce: Commercial Service, 19; Export Assistance Centers, 155

U.S. Department of Defense, 155–56; National Security Education Program, 155–56

U.S. Department of Education, 101, 111–12, 138, 141, 146–48; Business and International Education Program, Title VI-B, 101, 147; European Commission-United States Joint Consortia for Cooperation in Higher Education and Vocational Education, 148; Fulbright Group Projects Abroad Program, 146–47; Fulbright Seminars Abroad Program, 147; Fund for the Improvement of Postsecondary Education (FIPSE), 81–82, 87, 90, 148; International Education and Graduate Programs Service (IEGPS), 146–48; Program for North American Mobility in Higher Education, 148; Title VI-B Business Linkage Project, 74; Undergraduate International Studies and Foreign Language Program, 147–48; U.S.-Brazil Higher Education Consortia Program, 148

U.S. Department of State, 22, 29, 101, 106–7, 138, 141, 145, 148–55; Benjamin A. Gilman International Scholarship Program, 153; Bureau of Educational and Cultural Affairs, 148–55; Citizen Exchanges Program, 149; College and University Affiliations Program, 104; Community Connections Program, 149; Congress-Bundestag Exchange

Program, 149–50; Cooperative Grants Program, 150; Educational Partnerships Program, 150; English Language Fellows Program, 151; English Language Specialists Program, 151; Freedom Support Act Undergraduate Program, 151; Fulbright Occasional Lecturer Program, 151–52; Fulbright Scholar-in-Residence Program, 152; Fulbright Senior Specialist Program, 152; Fulbright Teacher and Administrator Exchange Program, 152–53; Fulbright U.S. Scholar Program, 153; International Visitors Program, 141, 153; National Clearinghouse on Disability and Exchange, 154; New Independent States College and University Partnership Program, 154; New Independent States Community College Partnership Program, 154; Overseas Education Information Centers, 154–55

U.S. Educational Information Center (Singapore), 95

U.S. immigrant students, 32; and ESL programs, 33–34

U.S. Information Agency (USIA), 72; University Affiliations Project, 74

U.S. Institute of Peace, 138–39

USAID University Linkage Project, 73, 76

Uzbekistan, and partnership programs, 154

V

Vaughan, George, 138

videoconferences, on international education, 140

Vietnam, Van Hien University (Ho Chi Minh City), 93

visiting scholars, federal funding for, 151–52

Vista University, Port Elizabeth campus (South Africa), 105–6

Vitale, Robert, xv

W

Web site, community college, as international recruitment tool, 21, 23

withdrawal rates, for international students, 37

Word Keys, 89

workforce, U.S., 8–9

workforce training, 156; COMPRO program, 82–87; through partnerships abroad, 99–100, 139

work-study programs, 84

world maps, displayed on campus, 131

writing instruction, in ESL programs, 35

Z

Zachary, G. Pascal, 6, 9

ABOUT THE EDITOR AND CONTRIBUTORS

Richard M. Romano is director of the Institute for Community College Research. He is a professor of economics and has been director of international education at Broome Community College (State University of New York) in Binghamton, New York, since 1979. In addition to his writings on international education and economics, he has written on general education.

Fay Beauchamp is professor of English at Community College of Philadelphia, where she is also coordinator of humanities and director of the Asian Studies Regional Center.

Audree M. Chase is a consultant on international education programs. She is former coordinator of international programs at the American Association of Community Colleges, Washington, D.C.

Allen Cissell is senior program officer, Community College Liaison Office, U.S. Department of Education, Washington, D.C.

Donald A. Dellow has been president of Broome Community College in Binghamton, New York, since 1988. He is active in the field of international education and has served on the board of directors of the College Consortium for International Studies and Community Colleges for International Development.

Jody Dudderar is the director of international programs and study abroad at SUNY Rockland Community College in Suffern, New York. She is on the board of directors of the College Consortium for International Studies and is a frequent conference presenter on study abroad.

Kent A. Farnsworth has served as president of Crowder College in Neosho, Missouri, since 1995. He is a nationally recognized speaker on globalizing the curriculum. In 1994, he was selected to participate in a Fulbright-Hays Fellowship in Pakistan and in 1996 was a Malone Fellow to the Kingdom of Saudi Arabia.

Robert A. Frost is an associate professor of International Studies at Parkland College, Champaign, Illinois.

William Greene has been director of international education at Broward Community College, Ft. Lauderdale, Florida, for more than 20 years. He has served in numerous leadership positions with the College Consortium for International Studies and has authored several articles on international education.

John Halder is the president of Community Colleges for International Development (CCID). The CCID central office is located at Kirkwood Community College in Cedar Rapids, Iowa.

Carolyn J. Kadel is faculty director of international education at Johnson County Community College in Overland Park, Kansas.

Linda A. Korbel is the executive director of the American Council on International Intercultural Education and dean of languages, humanities, and the arts at Oakton Community College, Des Plaines, Illinois.

David Levin is senior program manager in the U.S. Department of State's Bureau of Educational and Cultural Affairs, Washington, D.C. He has worked in the field of international education, in a variety of capacities, for the past 25 years.

Scott Branks del Llano is a professor in the World Languages, Cultures, and Communications Division at Richland College in Dallas, Texas. He teaches cultural studies and English as a second language and develops programs in global education, peace studies, and diversity.

Jeana Remington is the director of the American English and Culture Institute of the Dallas County Community College District. She coordinates curriculum and services to international students and develops programs in cultural studies and diversity.

Frank Schorn is the director of the Center for International Programs at Austin Community College in Austin, Texas. Earlier he worked for USAID and UNESCO in Asia, Africa, and the Caribbean.

Edward Stoessel is executive director of resource development/international and government relations at Eastern Iowa Community College District in Davenport, Iowa. He has been instrumental in the establishment of community college–based projects in a number of countries throughout the world.

Robert Vitale is the director of international education at Miami-Dade Community College in Miami, Florida. He is a member of the board of directors of the College Consortium for International Studies and is a frequent presenter at conferences on international education.